$2.96

The Touch of Friendship

# The Touch of Friendship

## HAROLD E. DYE

**BROADMAN PRESS**
Nashville, Tennessee

© Copyright 1979 • Broadman Press.
All rights reserved.

4254-22
ISBN: 0-8054-5422-5

Dewey Decimal Classification: 301.43
Subject heading: ELDERLY/FRIENDSHIP
Library of Congress Catalog Card Number: 79-51138
Printed in the United States of America.

# Preface

When I was first invited to write this book, my exact words were: "You've got the wrong pig by the ear. I am not a very sociable cuss." I was given a couple of weeks to think it over.

I made a speech at a Kiwanis Club recently. I was amazed to hear the master of ceremonies introduce me as "one of the most outgoing men" he had ever met. I did not dispute him but he damaged my speech. I kept thinking in the back of my mind about how dead wrong he was. I felt that I was sailing under false colors. I am not at all what I would call "outgoing." I am not what psychologists call "extroverted"—at least I don't think that I am.

All my life I have been troubled by a sort of crippling shyness. The psychologists pounce on that word *shy* like ducks on a June bug. They affirm that *shyness* is really self-centeredness. I have little doubt but that they are right. They say that the shy person tells himself that he is not good enough, that people won't like him, that they will think unkind thoughts about him. He sells himself short, both to himself and to his fellows. It follows, then, that one must accept himself for what he is before he can accept others for what they are.

It is precisely because I have had to work and am still working on many of the problems mentioned in this book that I finally decided to write it. I believe that I am more sensitive to the many heartaches, inconsistencies, and uncertainties in interpersonal relationships than are those who have never felt them.

For this reason, I have made the book very personal. I just ask that you take my hand and let us walk along together—being friends in spirit. Then, let us extend our hands to other pilgrims and find some joys in the rest of our lives that we may have missed before.

The frank admissions of my own weaknesses and failures fill some of these pages. Much of the book is humorous so that we may laugh together at me, and at each other. This is the way with friends. You may disagree with some of my statements. That, again, is the prerogative of true friends—to disagree and to argue with each other in a spirit of mutual consideration and love.

Many of the personal experiences contain vignettes—glimpses of famous people as seen in my own experience and through my eyes. God has been good to me. Through my many years as pastor, writer, editor, and because I was privileged to serve in many denominational positions in the Baptist state conventions where I have lived, as well as in five Southern Baptist Convention places of responsibility, I have had as personal friends some of the choicest people that he ever made.

Let us now begin tearing down the walls that separate us from our fellow pilgrims of the Way.

# Contents

1. Friends Are Where You Make Them . . .  9
2. "McGranahan's My Name—What's Yours?" . . . . . . . . . . . . . . . . . . . . .  21
3. Handshakes and Hugs . . . . . . . . . . . .  35
4. Say Yes to New Adventures. . . . . . . .  48
5. "Have I Told You About My Operation?"  66
6. A Merry Heart Doeth Good. . . . . . . . .  80
7. How to Be Dull Without Even Trying. . .  90
8. Watch Yourself Go By . . . . . . . . . . . .  102
9. Wear Your Age Proudly. . . . . . . . . . .  116
10. Koinonia . . . . . . . . . . . . . . . . . . . . .  130

# 1
# Friends Are Where You Make Them

High in the Sangre de Cristo Mountains of northern New Mexico, the Pecos River has its source. The Spanish conquistadores called this part of the Rocky Mountain chain, "Blood of Christ." From the west, the late afternoon sun washes the peaks with a somber red, and the devout Spaniards made the sign of the cross and looked upon them as a monument to Christ.

The eastern slopes are, for the most part, more gentle. From the air the tall firs, garnished with patches of golden aspens, are smooth and softened, a robe of green velvet, falling into gigantic folds. Pinned to the upper part of the robe are two sapphire jewels, winking and glimmering in the shifting light.

On the ground those jewels are discovered to be two exquisitely beautiful little lakes. Between them the Rio Pecos is born, nourished, and sent, first slowly, then quickly, on its tortuous way two thousand miles to sink into huge Lake Armistad, which washes the shores of Mexico. If on one side the great high peaks with their red hues are reminders of the blood of Christ, the other side can be faintly likened to another Bible picture. The Pecos carries the water of life to hundreds of thousands of thirsty acres which would be barren and unproductive without it. Far below the mountains where the land is flattened out, the Pecos irrigates fields of cotton, alfalfa, and crops of grain in New Mexico, Texas, and, released from their last imprisonment, the fields and gardens of Mexico.

The lakes where the river is born can be reached only by foot or on horseback, by federal permit to visit a wilderness area, and so remain in pristine beauty untouched by the mobs. More than fifty years have passed since I found them at the end of my trail and stood overcome by their startling beauty. The first lake, caught in the silver chalice of the eternities, is called Spirit—and no name could be more apt. The other matchless gem of glistening beauty, faceted by the fingers of God when the earth was young, is named after a man—Stewart. From these silver basins, tipped by the hand of the Creator, flow the crystal waters of the Rio Pecos. They gather speed as they tumble through the mountain gorge, singing a song that roars at times like the bourdon pipes of a giant organ. At other times, they whisper like the dulcies as they enter quiet pools to rest before beginning again their long journey.

The high waters of the upper Pecos have been a part of my life since I was thirteen years old. My father loved this land of rare beauty before me, and every vacation our family pitched our tent and set up primitive housekeeping where the song of the river could lull us to sleep at the close of the day. My father and I broke out bamboo rods, shouldered our split willow creels, and tried our best to outwit the fighting rainbow trout.

My father has been dead, now for forty-six years,

and my beautiful, fun-loving mother for more than half a century. My two brothers, John and Alfred, are gray-haired now and my pigtailed little sister, Eidra, has become a grandmother. Many things have changed, but the Pecos still tumbles down from the two sparkling lakes through a channel only imperceptibly deeper, untamed by any man-made dam across the canyon. May it ever be so!

My wife loves the Pecos country too. She does not know until she reads this, that up one branch canyon is an ancient aspen with a heart carved on its silver trunk. Within that heart, cut with a Barlow knife are two names, "Evelyn" and "Harold." *Her* name is Ina! Ah, but that was a long, long time ago when I was just fifteen. Through half a century of happy marriage, Ina and I have found our way back to the Sangre de Cristos and the tumbling waters of the Pecos.

So it came about that last summer we towed our little trailer up the winding road again. We intended to camp in our own special spot where the moss-covered bluffs rise high on one side and the stream washes the other edge of the rustic campground. As we came to the turn-off road, I shouted happily, "It's empty! Nobody here. We have it all to ourselves, just like we left it last year." I nosed the car into the entrance road.

Then I saw him. A man stepped out from the trees. Behind him was a trailer and a pickup truck. What was worse, there, where we had parked our trailer the year before, was another little "house on wheels." I was dismayed. Ina and I like to get off by ourselves—even where we will not see another person for a week or more. We have a four-wheel drive International Scout and can thus get into places where a conventional automobile cannot possibly go. I was about to suggest this to my equally disappointed wife when the stranger hailed us.

"Come on in," he said, "plenty of room. Park your rig and join us."

I had not climbed from the car; I still sat at the wheel in smouldering discontent, but the bluff, hearty stranger had come near and had thrust out his hand in welcome. Out of a clear blue sky he said, "The other couple and my wife and I are Baptists—hope you don't object."

The announcement was unexpected and I still do not quite understand why he made it. Though I was laughing inside, I fixed the man with a stern glance. "Baptists!" I said. "I would never admit it. Aren't you ashamed of yourselves?"

The man looked at me questioningly, and I laughed on the outside this time. "We, too, are Baptists and have been most of our lives. I guess if this is a Baptist camp we had better join it."

That is how Ina and I came to know Pete and Myra Reaves of Odessa, Texas, and Ed and Colleen Hale of Carlsbad, New Mexico. And if I had persisted in my bullheaded desire for privacy, we would have been immeasurably impoverished in spirit. We would have missed one of the dearest episodes of our lives.

That night Pete built a campfire on their site. He is a campfire builder than which there is no whicher. Over a handful of pungent shavings he built a little teepee of split wood. We gathered there, all six of us, just after darkness had enfolded the mountains. Pete knelt and a match flared. "Let there be light," he solemnly intoned, and there was light. Tongues of flame licked their way up the sides of the tiny teepee and there was a circle of light that shut out the rest of the world. Pete had suspended a ceiling of plastic over our heads. It was swung on a rope with its four corners tied to the branches of a tall pine. The transparent sheet reflected the heat downward and shooed the cold air currents away. We arranged our aluminum lawn chairs so we could face each other at will and just talked. Once a coyote yapped on a distant hill. At another time a skunk wandered into the light at the back of Pete's chair. Needless to say, we did not bother him but let him proceed on his unconcerned way, the white streak on his back wavering and twisting ghostlike in the fringe light.

All the while we just sat and talked, as thoughts came to us. We did not try to settle any of the world's problems and did not give a word to our own. The conversation was light, pleasant, and unhurried. And it was not carried on to the cacophonous background of a squawking television set. Only the whispering winds in the pine needles and the soft murmur of the nearby stream played harmonious obbligato to our spoken thoughts. Lasting friendships were born that night. We learned that Pete and Myra and Ed and Colleen had been strangers to each other just the week before. The Reaves couple had stayed in the campground once before, and, captured by its quiet beauty, had made their way back. Two days later the Hales scouted the place as a possible site to park their trailer. They had started to pull away when they saw the other trailer but Pete called to them. "Come on in; we are lonesome. We'd like a little company." They found out, quite by accident, that they shared common religious beliefs. It was probably in the exuberance of that discovery that Ed Hale communicated to me that unexpected information. Baptists are not all that plentiful in New Mexico, and especially in California where Ina and I make our home. Admittedly this was a bond that tied us closer together and made conversation easier, though I cannot remember that we talked about church at any time.

A few days later Ed and Colleen hitched their trailer to its towing vehicle. We shared a last cup of coffee together, and they pulled out. Before they did so, however, Ed gave me a couple of pieces of fishing equipment that he had purchased for use in a northern New Mexico lake which I intended fishing. We said warm good-byes and they were on their way with a friendly toot of the pickup's horn. The four of us, Pete and Myra, Ina and I, felt a little wave of sadness.

The next day Ina and I pulled out. As we said good-bye in the Reaves trailer, Pete's attractive wife, Myra, surprised me with a quick hug and a kiss on my leathery cheek. She gave my wife a half-gallon fruit jar filled with the juice of marble-sized chokecherries that she had gathered from a nearby mountainside, and they chatted a few moments about what turned out to be the making of delicious jelly. I shook hands with Pete and his eyes were a little misty, as were my own. And just one week before neither couple knew that the other even existed!

It would be easy for me to justify our initial attitude toward these strangers who had preempted our camping place. You would understand it perfectly as would any intelligent reader or listener.

We were in greater need of a rest than most people. My wife had lost her mother less than a month before. Ina's mother made her home with us the last year of her life. She was ninety-three years old when she died and her health had deteriorated until she was helpless. We dared not leave her alone. Finally came the long hospitalization during which time my wife spent many hours of every day at the bedside of her—and my own—precious little mother. When finally release came to her—and painfully to us—we felt it necessary to get away, to be alone with our hurt. We sandwiched vacation between speaking engagements for me where we would be surrounded by others for many days at a time.

I could summon other facts to our defense. We have many houseguests. We sometimes go for several months without being alone in our own home. This has simply been a fact of our life. We would have it no other way, but, still, there has been that inevitable nervous strain. It does not matter how congenial we all are, there is a certain drain on our energies.

There is another, and deeper, motivation. We have always loved the world of nature. The wilder the country, the more we like it. Through the years I have gone into the wilds for a week or more at a time where I saw no living soul—not even my own face except as it was mirrored in some quiet pool. In John Muir, Henry Thoreau, or the more modern Colin Fletcher *(The Man Who Walked Through Time)*, I find ready rapport. While Ina makes no such trips she still is happiest sitting with me by a lonely campfire far from the haunts of men. She has that delightful quality of companionship of not having to be entertained with constant conversation. She does not intrude upon my reflective moods—and I try (a little) not to trespass upon hers.

Yes, I could justify our seemingly cold and aloof attitude toward these strangers. You would understand perfectly. But the trouble is, I cannot justify it to my own soul. One thing I know: I would have cheated myself immeasurably had I not accepted Ed Hale's initial offer of friendship. Whether I would have cheated him is, of course, something I cannot really know. Ina and I gathered to ourselves jewels of beauty and golden threads of strength as we accepted the fellowship of four warmhearted pilgrims on life's tortuous way.

Nothing—absolutely nothing—takes the place of friendship. Gruff, old Samuel Johnson grew softly pensive as he called friendship "one of the greatest comforts of this earthly pilgrimage." With this all normal persons must agree. Then why do we not try to make more friends? Does the reason lie in the word *make?* Friends *do* have to be made, you know. They do not just happen. They are not accidental. They do not grow all by themselves. The seed has to be planted then carefully cultivated before we harvest such wondrous fruits of love.

We senior adults are living in the harvest years of life. Does that mean that we are to stop planting—desist from sowing seeds? Shall we let these later years lie fallow to reap a harvest of loneliness? We think not.

The late Bing Crosby had a song that he made famous called *Don't Fence Me In.* It is a Western song all about the barbed wire thrown across the great outreaches of land, sometimes as much as 125 square miles of open space. Sometimes surrounding as little as a lonely grave, it told the world to keep out. Most of us who were born and bred as Westerners share every sentiment of this lyrical protest against our physical freedom. We don't like it when we come to a stretch of five-wire barricade, especially when a placard may proclaim as many of them do: "No Trespassing—Survivors Will Be Shot." That is the way most of us feel whether we live in the East, West, North, or South. But we build our own fences, do we not? They are fences around our own souls. The tragedy is that we can't even see such fences. We wonder why we have so few friends. We do not realize that those who would be our friends are warned to keep out by our attitudes, our habits, and our almost complete inaccessibility.

My wife and I had thrown a mental fence around a beautiful spot on the Pecos River and had said to all others, "no trespassing." This was not a physical fence because we owned not one foot of the land. We could not throw bristling barbed wire around something which did not belong to us. But we did something much worse. We threw a spiritual fence around our own hearts and said to those who would have walked life's trail with us even for a little while: Do not disturb.

There is nothing wrong with our wanting to be alone at times. We need to do so. Even Jesus said to his disciples, "Come ye yourselves apart into a desert place, and rest a while" (Mark 6:31). We need time for meditation, for personal inventory, for rest, and peace where we can achieve harmony within ourselves. That is good for interludes, but it is not the main theme. As a way of life, it is deadly. We can be alone without being lonely. On this psychologists are agreed and our experience confirms it. On the other hand, if we insist upon too much "aloneness" and sow the seeds of personal isolation, we shall inevitably reap the whirlwind of loneliness, and it will twist our souls in the throes of a living death.

Yes; we all build spiritual fences around ourselves, and while they shut us in, they shut our neighbor out. I have always had trouble with one personal fence and as I grow older, I find myself building it more and more often. It is the fence of *independence*.

Many years ago I was helping my friend, Mickey Shannon, build a cabin for himself. Keep in mind it was *his* cabin that we were building. In my lifetime I had built three other cabins in the woods, so I had that experience behind me. I knew just how it should be done, and I jumped ahead of Mickey to do it. Finally, in exasperation, my friend complained, "You won't let me help you enough. Don't you know that I want to? That I need to learn from you? You are really kicking me off the floor of my own cabin." Mickey is now dead, but every time I see his cabin I think that I can hear his plaintive voice, "Why?"

As we grow older we are prone to guard our independence more jealously. We do not ask for help and when it is offered, we cannot accept it graciously. We are not only robbing ourselves but also we are cheating our friend out of something he needs. He needs to give of himself; we all do at whatever age.

I once was walking in a park with a group of people. We were one by one crossing a stream on a log. Just in front of me was a little, white-haired woman. Suddenly the log shook. I reached quickly to grab my little companion's arm. She shook my hand off, whirled toward me, and said, "I don't need your help!" In turning to confront me, she lost her balance, fell to the ground beneath, and broke her hip. In a matter of six weeks her injury had healed. For forty years I have carried a wound in my heart. I have asked myself, Did I cause her to fall? Did I inadvertently push her off balance? I cannot know for sure the answer to the questions but I do know this: She took away from me a simple pleasure—that of being able to help her—and she thus left me with a pain that simply could not be put in a plaster cast.

I have mentioned harmony of our own spirits. Such harmony can come to us only when we are in harmony with those around us. No one of us can make melody when he has only one note called "I."

This book has just one aim: to cause the reader (and the writer) to reach out to others; to continue to be a part of the stream of life; to come out of our shells, or not to retire within them; to make and to *be* friends.

My wife and I have a rustic cabin in the High Sierras of California. It is an old-fashioned sort of place with wood-burning stoves, water hauled from the creek, and no fence around it. Across the front door of our cabin is the kind of lock our forefathers used. A heavy oak bar is hinged on a steel bolt at one end. The other end drops into a notch in a matching piece of oak. Once the bar is in place the cabin is secure from all intruders. One end of a rawhide thong passes through the bar and through a hole above it, then hangs on the outside of the door. When that rawhide string is on the outside anyone can get into the cabin without a key. When the thong is pulled back through the hole on the inside, the door would have to be broken down before entrance could be made. Most of the time the latchstring on our cabin door is out. Some of our friends feel free to pull it without knocking.

Is the latchstring of your heart on the outside? Can a friend find his way into your heart without knocking? Remember that no one who would become your friend will ever try to climb over the wall you may have built around yourself.

# 2
# "McGranahan's My Name— What's Yours?"

I met McGranahan nearly forty years ago. I just shook hands with him. I would not know him now if I saw him, but he made an impression on me that I never tried to shake off.

Two letters landed on my desk in the same mail. One of them is the kind that almost every pastor gets now and then. They also get the other kind once in awhile, but not often enough. It is a strain on credulity that both kinds of letters came to me in the same mail. That's why I remember the incident so well.

Any pastor will recognize the first letter. It starts innocently enough:

Dear Sir:
On our recent visit to the West, we visited your church. This is to inform you that we found it to be the most unfriendly, cold church that we have ever been in. Not a living soul shook hands with us except the pastor, and we had to shake hands with him to get out the front door.

But the other letter, ah, and shure it wahrms the cockles of your heart, it does. It was signed "J. J. McGranahan." "Dear Pastor," it read, "I have just returned from a business trip out West. Two weeks ago I was in your evening service. I liked it all. I liked your sermon, Reverend. But what I liked the most was that friendly bunch of people. I never in all my days met more warmhearted Christians."

I read the two letters and then leaned back in my desk chair and thought about McGranahan. I have been thinking about him off and on these forty years.

The night he visited our church I was sitting in the church parlor listening to a Training Union program. It was summertime and the windows were open. Ours was an old-fashioned brick building with a half basement and wide concrete stairs leading up from both sides to the auditorium.

Suddenly our Training Union program was interrupted by a booming voice on the stairs outside.

"McGranahan's my name. What's yours?"

Since I was near the window, I peeked outside. A huge, red-faced Irishman had hemmed up one of our more diffident church members against the brick balustrade and was vigorously pumping his hand. They walked up the steps together, but on the middle landing the big voice boomed again: "McGranahan's my name. What's your?" And I knew that another one of our members was shaking hands with the genial Irishman.

A few weeks later I received another letter. It was from a pastor in a neighboring state. It seems that the Sunday School director of his church had visited our church services and had found our people to be most unfriendly. No one, he claimed, had spoken to him except the pastor. With admirable brotherly concern, the other pastor concluded, "I thought you might appreciate this information."

Since the pastor gave the name of his church and its location, it was easy for me to remember something that he could not possibly know. I had called attention to the presence of this same Sunday School director on the morning that he visited our congregation and had extended to him a public welcome.

Just as the service was over, this particular visitor had dashed from the building as though his pants were on fire! If I had not asked someone else to lead the benediction while I tiptoed back to the foyer, not even I could have shaken hands with this worshiper. I could not blame my people. Who wants to run the risk of shaking hands with a fellow in that big a rush to get away from the scene? One might get his hand jerked off in the process.

Do you ever feel that the people in a church that you visit are unfriendly? For that matter, do you sometimes feel that the people everywhere you go are unfriendly toward you? That they care nothing about you? That they would rather not even be bothered by you? Try a little experiment. Remember McGranahan. Take the initiative. Stick out your hand, announce your own name, and see what happens. You will be pleasantly surprised.

I do not know where my Irish friend McGranahan is now. I may have to wait until I get to heaven to hear him shout, "McGranahan's my name!" (if we have to introduce ourselves there). Of one thing I am certain. If McGranahan is still alive, he never visits an unfriendly church.

He makes certain of that.

# The *Real* George Truett

At the invitation of District Missionary Lowell Ponder, I was the pastor for the District Four Texas Youth Encampment at beautiful Palacios-by-the-Sea, for five straight years. During a break in the meetings, John Shepard, pastor of the First Baptist Church in Angleton, Texas, and I drove down to Galveston to fish. This was shortly after the death of George W. Truett, considered to be one of the greatest preachers on the earth.

We sat on the spray-drenched jetty, lazily casting our lines out into the white surf of the Gulf of Mexico. We were trying for speckled trout. Just beyond our farthest casts the porpoises played, gracefully chasing each other as they slithered in and out of the water like huge sea serpents fully two feet in diameter and scores of feet long.

John leaned back against a slab of concrete. His straw hat was cocked over one eye, and his dark glasses were clouded even more by the salt mist. Now and then he pulled in his line for inspection. As is the way with preachers, we were discussing people, especially other preachers, their foibles, their whims, their fancies, and their shortcomings, nothing more serious than our common weaknesses. In particular, we were paying our respects to some preachers who like to bask in the limelight, even if that limelight happens to be surrounding another.

Shepard pulled in his line and critically examined it. "I was on a train one time," he said, deftly flipping his bait back into the water, "on my way to an evangelistic conference. Besides me," he added with a sly little grin, "there were other great men on that train, one of whom was George W. Truett, seated up front reading a newspaper. A pompous brother entered the coach, and, noticing the empty seat by the pastor of the First Baptist Church of Dallas, as you know, the largest Baptist church in the world, he strolled over to it, making sure that the eyes of the other brethren were upon him.

" 'Good morning, Dr. Truett, I am Reverend Blank!' Without an invitation, he sat down by Truett.

"Dr. Truett, who was always courteous, acknowledged the introduction and turned back to his newspaper.

"The pompous preacher was enjoying the impression he thought he was making on us hoi polloi. He kept leaning over to Dr. Truett, making some hopefully wise observations to which his illustrious seatmate would make some noise deep down in his throat like 'harumph' and keep right on reading.

"After about thirty minutes of this, the persecuted Truett got up, thrust his paper into his pocket, excused himself, and walked slowly down the aisle, nodding to friends right and left.

"In the seat ahead of me sat a young fellow, who, I learned later, had just been ordained to the gospel ministry. Apparently, he knew no one on the train. He sat alone, fingering a book, and staring mostly out the window.

"Dr. Truett spied the young man and dropped down beside him. I could not help eavesdropping any more that you could have," continued Shepard apologetically. "And I am glad that I did, for what I heard was a greater sermon for me than any I had ever heard that great man of God deliver from the pulpit. It was an exquisite example of love and friendship—worth more than a whole book on the subject.

" 'Good morning,' he said, 'My name is George W. Truett.' Think of that! Here that poor kid preacher sat almost worshiping the master pulpiteer of his lifetime, whose picture was just about everywhere—and George Truett was actually introducing himself as though he were an equal . . . hold it, I've got a strike!" He failed to hook the fish, and excused himself to me for missing. "I was so interested in my story that I wasn't watching my business . . . ."

"Get on with it, Man," I said, excitedly.

"Well, that young preacher stammered out his own name. Soon they were chatting like a couple of schoolboys . . . . I've got another strike!" John reeled in a beautiful "spec" and flopped it over at my feet. He rebaited his hook and got to his feet. As he leaned over to follow through on his cast, he said, "You know, they have tried to put George Truett on a phonograph record. Pshaw! You might as well try to put this gulf in a teaspoon. You can buy a recorded sermon of Truett and play it in church, but the real George Truett is recorded on human hearts. No phonograph record could ever capture his simple love, or his contempt for sham."

"Amen," I whispered, for I was thinking about the time George Truett put his arm around me when, as a very young preacher, I was introduced to him. "I shall add you to my prayer list, Harold," he said, "for I pray for every young preacher that I chance to meet. May our God watch over you."

My eyes were misty with a salt not brought by the Gulf breeze as we arose to leave the jetty.

## What's *Your* Name?

I have never cared much for the sound of my last name. Too many other words rhyme with Dye—lie, sly, pie, and so on. Many a budding school poet has tried a hand at my name with what were, to me, nonlaughable results. When our children were babies, it was not at all uncommon for some Bob Hope type to accost me with, "How's Mrs. Dye and all the little Dy-pers?"

My antipathy toward my first name is also easily aggravated. I have never liked the name Harold—for me, that is. What is more, I have met many other Harolds who have resented the fact that so many comic strips and movies have made the bumbling fool a "Harold." I like to read Ann Landers, in spite of the fact that so many times she lets her prejudice get in front of her wisdom. Most of us appreciate that she is not afraid to assert herself on the matter of sexual decency. But I almost swore off her the other day. A woman had complained about her son-in-law's eating habits. He "eats like a pig," she said. Her young son was beginning to copy the "pig's" boorish table habits. Ann Landers assured the complainer, whose name was *Tired of Looking the Other Way in Louisville,* that a twenty-two-year-old man who eats like a pig is not about to be retrained. She suggested that the woman have a heart-to-heart talk with her young son: "Sample: Harold is a very fine young man . . . ." Who was Harold? The Pig!

Some of us Harolds are getting so tired of this that we are thinking of organizing a combine called "Harolds Anonymous Against the World." I have always liked my middle name better, but Eldon Dye sounds like a bouncing Ping-Pong ball. So, I am stuck with Harold. At least it is better than being called by my Social Security number all the time—"Hi, there, 564-64-1084!"

Silly as my name sounds to me, I have found it useful in getting acquainted with others. Once I stuck out my hand to a man in a corridor of the First Baptist Church in Fairbanks, Alaska.

I said, "Dye."

Quicker than the smash of Wyatt Earp's forty-five, the man answered, "Deadman." It was as though my trigger finger had dropped the hammer on my own revolver, and I had shot him squarely through the heart. We both laughed. Our improbable names had launched us on a rewarding friendship. Alaska at that time was not even a state. I was a stranger in a strange place, but the "dead" man led me from one church member to another, introducing me and warning them that I was trigger-happy and had shot him with my loaded finger. Everyone laughed. I was a stranger no longer. Furthermore, I was in a friendly land. I might not have learned this had I been too timid to offer my hand and my name.

One of the first things to be learned in all social contacts is to get the other person's name right. We are all touchy on that point. I have implied that I do not care too much for the ribald use of my first name or the way my last name sounds. Nevertheless, if my name is used, I want it spelled right. You feel the same way about yours. I joined an association for the retired. On every letter they sent to me my name was spelled "Dyr." I protested in vain. How can you argue with a computer? Finally I got a bill for my dues. It was on an IBM card (do not spindle, bend, or mutilate). I folded the card in three places and sent it back with another letter of protest about my misspelled name. That did it. The machine kicked me out into the lap of a bookkeeper. I report now that my name is Har*a*ld Dye instead of Harold. I report, also, that Harald Dye, alias Dyr, has not yet paid his dues.

So, you see, even though I have ambivalence about my names, I am not ambivalent about the spelling of them.

Whatever *your* name is, you want it spelled and pronounced right. What's more, you will not like the person who does not do so—ever. We should apply our sensitivity to our own names to the names of others.

In the first place, we compliment an individual when we remember that person's name—especially after a single contact. Every individual that you will ever meet is unique. There is not another exactly like that one on the earth. (There's no one exactly like you, either, and you can remember that with pride.) Since each of us is unique, each is entitled to his identification by name and not just as a number in a computer system.

Contrariwise, we insult the other fellow when we forget his name. He will probably be too much gentleman to show it, but he will feel it. Suffice it to say (and I keep on learning the lesson by painful experience) you can never win friends and influence people by forgetting their names. Ask Dale Carnegie. He wrote the book.

When you hear a name offered in introduction, make sure that you get it right the first time. Ask the name over if you, like me, are hard of hearing in times of confusing noise. Of course, if President Jimmy Carter introduces you to his security adviser—forget it, or just sneeze. Who could spell or remember Zbigniew Brzezinski? On the other hand, if you have a mind like mine, you would probably remember how to spell that and forget how to spell John Smith.

Any news reporter learns quickly (and sadly) that if he writes any person's name, however unusual that name might be, he had better get it right, every jot and tittle of it or his own name will be Mud. Back in the days when I served as a denominational editor, Southern Baptists had a great leader named Hight C Moore. He served as editorial secretary of the Sunday School Board of the Southern Baptist Convention. Dr. Moore was a noted writer and was a gracious and loving man. I knew him personally and my admiration for him was unbounded. It so happened that the middle name of Hight Moore was C. That was the whole name. We editors learned to watch any story about Hight C Moore written by an associate to make certain that no period was put after the middle C of Hight C Moore.

Richard Buckminster Fuller, Jr. is a designer, inventor, philosopher, father of the geodesic dome, and author of many books. Most of those who hear his name for the first time stare in astonishment. Some of the more courageous simply say, "I'll just call you Bucky." Now, I have never met the gentleman and never expect to, but I wonder how he feels about such sacrilege. I venture to say it rattles his geodesic dome.

Something else rattles my own dome. If I have not seen you in a century or so, please do not come up to me and say, "You don't know me, do you?" and stare me in the eye. Because I am likely to say, "Sorry, I do not. I do not remember that I have ever seen you before." Of course, being a person of culture, you would never do such a thing.

My wife and I had a delightful experience last fall. We attended a reunion of former students of Montezuma Baptist College near Las Vegas, New Mexico.

The meeting was held in beautiful Chaparral Inn at the Glorieta Conference Center. It was attended by seventy-five alumni of the little college that closed its doors in 1932.

Have you ever walked into a room filled with people whom you knew well fifty years before and most of whom you had not seen since? Of course *you* have not changed in all those years but everyone else has—and how! There were about a half dozen of our old classmates whom we had seen in all that time, therefore, we could only recognize them; the others seemed to be total strangers.

Ina and I were married at Montezuma in 1927. Such marriages were against college regulations. I prevailed upon the president of the college, Dr. C. R. Barrick, to perform the ceremony that united us in marriage. The wedding took place in the home of my bride's parents. Her father was employed by the college.

President Barrick pronounced us husband and

wife and then tapped me on the shoulder. "You have a date with me in my office tomorrow morning," he said. The next day he lowered the boom on us. We were expelled for getting married as we were certain we would be.

The very first one that we saw at the Montezuma rally was Dr. Barrick, who had married us fifty years before and then clobbered us! I am glad to say that he had not changed a bit. He was just as trim as ever, though he did ache a little after Ina and I got through hugging him.

One interesting thing about this meeting was that not one person walked up to another with the inane question, "You don't know me, do you?" Each introduced himself as though none of us had ever met before. There was no embarrassment, no strain. But there was plenty of love. The years flew from us like dew before the sun, and we were all young again.

Have you ever noticed someone coming your way who seemed to be vaguely familiar to you, yet you could not, for the life of you, remember his name? You asked yourself in a panic, "What will I do?" Then, as you met, that person smiled and said, "Hi. I'm so and so," and your relief almost choked you? That is an unmistakable mark of courtesy.

### Pride in Your Own Name

On a previous page, I joked some about my own name, just to illustrate a point. Actually I am very proud of my family name. It belonged to the man whom I loved more than any other man I ever knew: my father, Harvey Smith Dye. My dad was a sensitive, intelligent, loving individual. He never made much impression except upon those who came to know him. He had a good library of worthwhile books and taught me to like good literature. He was a fine violinist, one of the first to play over the "wireless," as we called the radio.

When I was about a dozen years old, Dad and I went mountain hiking in the Sandias, near Albuquerque. We sat on a high overlook, our eyes drifting over the heads of tall firs and lower pines and aspens on to the far horizon. Dad turned to me and laid his hand on my arm.

"Son," he said, "I can't leave you much when I die. All that I have is a little house and a beat-up old car. Your precious mother's sickness took all the money I had saved up and will take all my extra money for, perhaps, more years than I shall live. About all that I can really leave you is my name. I have tried to keep it honorable and clean. Promise me now that you will do the same."

Our hands met in a solemn pact there on a mountain crest so long ago. I have tried to keep my promise to my earthly father and to the heavenly Father who witnessed it.

We are proud of our names, and why shouldn't we be? They are names that are on the family roll of God.

## The Name Above All Names

One day, when spiritual darkness covered the land, an angel appeared to Joseph, the son of David, the husband of Mary, who was yet a virgin. The angel spoke away the disquiet in the heart of Joseph, the just man. The angel told him that Mary had been touched by the Holy Spirit, had conceived, and would bear a son: "And thou shalt call his name

Jesus: for he shall save his people from their sins" (Matt. 2:21).

This is the Name of names: Jesus. The Word of God says: "There is none other name under heaven given among men, whereby we must be saved" (Acts 4:12).

This book is directed to those who follow Jesus. We live to one purpose: to introduce our Lord and Savior to others. Most of us have grown old in his service. We have walked a long trail with him. We know beyond the peradventure of any doubt that he has never failed us. He has never forsaken us. He has never let us down. He has lifted our feet from the path of destruction and has guided them along the pathway of eternal life. Then why should any one of us retire within his own soul and shut out the one who would find Christ through us? It is unthinkable.

We shall grow old—if we live at all. We shall grow weak—if we walk at all. We shall talk softly—if we talk at all. But as long as we have breath, we can speak the name of Jesus and our hearts and lives will be radiant; our last days on the earth will be better than our first.

"Wherefore God also hath highly exalted him, and given him a name which is above every name: That at the name of Jesus every knee should bow, of things in heaven, and things in earth, and things under the earth; And that every tongue should confess that Jesus Christ is Lord, to the glory of God the Father" (Phil. 2:9-11).

# 3
# Handshakes and Hugs

I do not come from a Baptist background. As a child I went, with my parents, to the First Christian Church of Tulsa, Oklahoma. The distinguished pastor of the church in those days was Dr. Meade C. Dutt. He is one of my favorite sermonizers even today. My people in the Cookson Hills of Oklahoma belonged, for the most part, to the Church of Christ. They still believe that I am on my way to hell on doctrinally greased skids. When I first began attending the First Baptist Church of Albuquerque, New Mexico, in my early teens, my sweet mother was upset. "If you join that church, I can't even take the Lord's Supper with you," she said, and it troubled me. She died never knowing that I had become a Baptist preacher. She never heard me preach. That is why I waited a full six months after my salvation before joining the church. I might never have done so except for a handshake.

My high school friend, Peris Woodruff, invited me to attend revival services at the church and in that very first meeting I confessed Christ as my Savior. I attended Sunday School, BYPU, and even sang in the choir but would not be baptized.

At that time the pastor of First Baptist Church

was Dr. T. F. Harvey. He was the best expository preacher I have ever heard. In fact, he was such a doctrinal teacher that, when at age nineteen, the church ordained me to preach the gospel, I passed the examination without ever cracking a book—not even the Bible. (With Dr. C. W. Stumph, the state corresponding secretary leading the questioning, that was quite an accomplishment.) I made only one mistake. I said that the Bible commanded us to observe the Lord's Supper every Sunday (my Disciples' background). My rigid questioner asked, drily, "Where?"

Though I loved hearing T. F. Harvey preach, I was afraid of him. So, too, were most of the other young people of the church. He drove a Model T Ford like the biblical Jehu, "furiously." He flaunted ministerial tradition (black ministerial garb) by wearing a white linen vest in the pulpit. He had a way of hooking his thumbs in its armholes, fixing his eyes on the right corner of the ceiling, and turning loose such theological blasts that the very devils cried out for mercy. Dr. Harvey preached without notes, but he did not look at his congregation unless there was some minor disturbance. Then, when he fixed those little eyes of his on the face of the offender, something in that unfortunate person's head snapped. I know.

Take one example. There were five young men of whom the church was particularly proud for a certain reason. All were students at Montezuma Baptist College. All were volunteers for special service. During a holiday season, four of the students came home and attended worship services on Sunday morning. As I recall it, Russell Goff, Peris Woodruff, Tom Wiley, and I were these ill-fated students. Tom later became a noted educator, serving as superintendent of education for the state of New Mexico most of his adult life. The other three became successful pastors.

We were seated in the annex of the old building at Broadway and Lead that Sunday morning. The annex was used for Sunday School but a sliding partition made it a part of the auditorium for the preaching service. At the front end of the annex was the baptistry. Near the baptistry on the front row always sat Deacon L. O. Anderson. He was a Swede—a wonderful man of God. His head was bald as a peeled onion.

This sad Sunday morning we four ministerial hopefuls, who were supposed to be lapping up the drippings from the sanctuary, lost all interest in the pastor's sermon. We were enthralled by the antics of a big, black spider. It lowered itself from the ceiling with spasmodic jerks. We saw that it would land squarely on the old deacon's head. Slowly the evil-looking black arachnid jerked its way toward the bald head glowing invitingly in the light of the blazing cross behind the baptistry. We held our breaths in excitement.

Suddenly the spider touched down. The beloved deacon flinched then lifted his huge hand and slapped it down on his head with an audible splat. In that split second all four of us let out our breaths at the same time and from one of the aspiring theologues came a blasting "Wow!"

The sound from the pulpit stopped. Dr. Harvey looked our way and astonishment was written on his face. The astonishment quickly gave way to anger. He fixed us with those flashing black eyes and said not one word. Then, after an eternity, he shouted, "The services will continue after the four young men who are creating the disturbance in the annex leave the building." All eyes turned our way. It was the longest walk I ever took.

I told you that so you could see that we young people had every reason to fear the displeasure of the pastor.

Now, back to my story:

I had been trying to sing bass in the choir for six months after my profession of faith. One Sunday morning the pastor finished his sermon, turned, and walked back toward his study. He did this frequently. It was as though he had drained himself physically and emotionally and had to sit down. This particular time, I was standing at the end of the choir loft when the pastor brushed past me on his way to the door to his private sanctuary. As he passed by me, he quickly reached behind his back and caught my hand in a warm grip. I was startled. First, I wondered how he had unerringly found my hand without looking around. Did he have gimlet eyes in the back of his head too? Then I asked myself the important question: Why? The question seemed to answer itself: Because he loved me as a person, because he cared.

Impulsively I followed the pastor into his study. He gave me a broad smile which lighted up his tired face and indicated a chair at the end of his desk. We talked until long after the lunch hour. That night I presented myself for membership in one of the greatest churches on the earth.

This is what *one* loving handshake can do.

By the way, when we four "spider watchers" apologized to Brother Harvey for interrupting his sermon, he threw back his head and laughed uproariously. We were never afraid of him again.

Jehu, the "fast driver" mentioned before, was also a handshaker. He was the avenger who killed the wicked Jezebel and the prophets of Baal and restored some order to Israel. There is an interesting note to this bloody story. Leaving Samaria, he saw Jehonadab coming to meet him. He saluted the son of Rechab and asked him, "Is thine heart right, as my heart is with thy heart? And Jehonadab answered, It is." Then the warrior said, "If it be, give me thine hand" (2 Kings 10:15).

Is not this, after all, what the handshake is all about? It is the symbol of joined hearts. It is a seal of friendship. Perhaps nothing we do or say better expresses our personality than does our simple handclasp.

During the early years of my ministry, I idolized an author who was well-known for his iconoclastic, hard-hitting books. He attacked with forensic fury atheistic, communistic professors who were teaching in our colleges. In 1933 he authored a book about "vanishing virgins." In all that he wrote, he pulled no punches. I admired his style and was certain that in addition to his undeniably keen mind, he must also be a "two-fisted" man.

On my first trip to California, I tried to locate the publishing house that produced his books. It was supposedly located in San Diego. I never found it. I was interested in getting to know this powerful writer.

Years passed. While I was editor of *The Baptist*

*New Mexican* in Albuquerque, an author came to town to speak in a certain church. I heard him speak then went forward to meet him. I don't know what I said to him, but I do know his lisping answer, run all together: "Isthetso?" (Translation: "Is that so?") He said it as though he was trying to spit. I also remember his handshake. It was like taking hold of a dead fish. Years passed and that author was shot in California by a husband who resented his intimacies with the husband's pretty wife. Now I know that this defies all logic, but I was not at all surprised! I had already decided in my own mind that the man's handshake revealed him to be a fake. Two-fisted man, indeed! He may have been a wow with the ladies, but, after that fishy handshake, he was a big nothing to me.

So, you see, we judge one another by our handshakes. You have shaken enough hands to know that I am right. Do you remember that patronizing woman who handed you two limp fingers from a dainty arm bent like the neck of a goose? How could you ever forget her? You'd like to, though. Do you remember the other woman who took your hand and held it—and held it—and held it—until you wanted to yell, "If you are through playing with my hand, will you please give it back? I have to go now and would like to take it with me." How about the burly bruiser who took your hand and tried to crush it in a vise-like grip? And there's the fellow who had one finger doubled up in some secret sign and all that you got was a squeeze on his knuckle.

On the positive side, there are women who can shake your hand and caress your heart at the same time. I like that kind of woman. Any man likes that kind of woman. Any woman likes that kind of woman. How do they do it? They *feel* close to you and express that feeling in the genuine warmth of a simple clasping of hands.

There are men whose strength reaches out to you in their firm grip of your hand. You are reassured; your faith in your fellowman has been renewed; you are better simply because they communicated to you their interest and their love. Because, you see, we all need the touch of another.

The late R. G. Lee in his book, *The Name Above Every Name,* exhausts the alphabet in his descriptive names for Christ. When he gets to *T* he says: "He is the Teacher, Truth, Tabernacle, Testator, Treasure, Tree of Life." I hope that Dr. Lee would have forgiven me, but I would like to add another *T.* He is the Toucher.

A poor leper knelt before the Master and cried out, "If thou wilt, thou canst make me clean. And Jesus, moved with compassion, put forth his hand, and touched him, and saith unto him, I will; be thou clean" (Mark 1:40-41).

Think of it! This unfortunate man had been forced to pull his tattered robe around himself when anyone passed by and cry out, "unclean! unclean!" lest they be contaminated by a contact with his sores. He had probably gone many years without feeling the touch of another's hand. Then, marvel of marvels, the Man from Galilee touched him—actually *touched* him. In that blessed moment Jesus not only took away the man's disease but he took away his loneliness too.

Jesus went about doing good the Bible says. In

that process, he went about touching people. Jesus touched the hand of Peter's wife's mother and the fever fled from before his gentle fingers. He touched the eyes of blind men and they could see. He touched the ears and the tongue of the man who could neither hear nor speak, and the man was no longer an object of pity. He touched the little children, and they were blessed. He touched the disciples on the mountaintop and Peter, James, and John were no longer afraid. He touches each of us in the dark night of the soul, and *we* are no longer afraid.

The very least that we as Christians can do is to pass on the touch of Jesus. I believe it was Evangeline Booth herself who told how she noticed coming into the Salvation Army mission where she was conducting services, a woman whose sinful profession seemed to be written on her face. She was a painted woman from the streets. She sat staring defiantly while the Salvation Army leader spoke from the Word of God. At the close of the service, the gentle Evangeline Booth made her way to the woman, stooped, and quickly kissed her on the cheek. The woman from the street lifted her faltering fingers to the spot on her cheek. "You kissed me," she whispered. She had not felt a holy kiss in a score of years. The touch of Evangeline Booth's saintly lips to the face of the toughened woman led her to exclaim, "Oh, show me the Christ who can make a woman like you!"

I was helping my friend Sam Jones in a revival in Lancaster, California. Our routine visiting was interrupted one afternoon by an urgent call from the hospital. One of his church members was very ill. Sam and I jumped in his car, and we sped to the hospital at the edge of town. Sam whirled his car into the parking lot and the only open parking spaces were marked "Doctor." There were at least six of them. As we stepped out of the car, an attendant confronted us. "Only doctors can park there!" he said. "I know," said Sam, "and I am in a hurry. Here, park my car a little better and leave the keys on the seat. I have to see a patient." I could hardly contain my laughter.

"You are a mean, tough man," I said, "you made that poor guy think you were a doctor." My friend Sam just grinned.

We made our call, prayed with the woman, and left as soon as we could. As we passed the visitors' room on our way out, Sam stopped abruptly. He moved quickly into the waiting room and dropped down on one knee before a little flaxen-haired girl. He caught her tiny hand in his big one. The little one was sitting alone. Her eyes were wide and hurt and questioning. A tear glistened on her cheek.

Sam reached into his breast pocket, took out his handkerchief, and carefully wiped away the tear. "There, Sweetheart," he said, "is someone you love sick?"

"They have taken Mummy upstairs, somewhere. She is sick. She told me to wait here."

"Are you afraid?" the pastor asked, gently.

"Not anymore," she smiled bravely. "You took my scared away."

Sam Jones threw his muscular arms around the little tyke and gave her a big hug. "Everything will be all right," he said. He stood to his feet, all six-feet-five of him.

The little girl looked up at him towering above

her and the smile that she gave him melted him down to her size.

"You *are* the best doctor in the house," I said, as we walked out to the parking lot.

Whether five years old or fifty, we all need someone's arms around us.

I can remember some hugs that I have received from men. These were great men who threw their arms around me. I cannot help but feel that those loving embraces greatly influenced my life.

In the preceding chapter I mentioned that, as a young preacher, I had felt George Truett's arms around me. Actually it happened twice, then and in later life when I served with that extraordinary man on the old Relief and Annuity Board of the Southern Baptist Convention. The first time was at the Paisano Baptist Encampment in the Davis Mountains of Texas. My wife, a fellow pastor, and I had driven down from our home in New Mexico. George Truett was the preacher for this "cowboy" camp meeting. I am sure that when Truett preached at this meeting and at the nearby Bloys Campground, he was at his very best. Cattlemen especially loved him.

After the last service of the Paisano meeting, my pastor friend, Bill Bolton, who knew Truett well, insisted on taking me up to the platform and introducing me. Truett impulsively hugged me to his broad chest and assured me of his continued prayers for me, but he added a specific one. "Now, Harold, since you will be driving back home tonight, be extra careful. I'll be praying for your safety."

We drove back through Marfa, and about ten miles beyond, suddenly I saw the fiery glare of eyes in the road. I threw on the brake and the car came to a screeching stop—almost. Now, that automobile was an old-time narrow gauge Willys. It was little more than a death trap at best.

I never knew where that 2,000 pound bull came from, but he charged *us*. He hit the front end of the car and smashed the radiator back against the engine. He shook his head dazedly and charged back into the night.

The thought has persisted through the years: Did the prayers of George Truett save our lives?

A short time later, I preached in an associational meeting in El Paso. Sitting on the front row right before me was Dr. J. B. Tidwell, the noted Bible expositor. His presence made me nervous, and I tried not to look at him while I spoke. My worry was baseless. When I closed my message, Dr. Tidwell was on his feet. He stepped up on the low platform and threw his arms around me. "Boy, you are on fire!" he said, "Never let that fire go out!"

There are two more personal examples that I feel constrained to mention as illustrative of the lasting influence of a warm, affectionate hug.

While I was pastor in Las Cruces, New Mexico, I built a cabin on the Ruidoso River in the mountains in the central part of the state. The assembly grounds of New Mexico Baptists were located there. Dr. L. R. Scarborough, president of Southwestern Baptist Seminary, was a frequent speaker at the assembly. He stayed in the beautiful lodge which had been given to him by his cattleman brother, W. F. Scarborough. The lodge was located about one mile upriver from our cabin.

One afternoon I paid a call on L. R. Scarborough.

I do not remember why I did so. He was at his typewriter, writing his book, *Products of Pentecost*. Before I left, this tremendous exponent and preacher of the Word insisted that I read the pages of his book that had just come from his typewriter. I was astonished and flattered. Mine were the second pair of eyes—his own first—to read those words. I voiced my enthusiasm. Dr. Scarborough, who knew that I had neither finished college nor seminary, gravely thanked me, his twenty-eight-year-old friend. Then, as I said good-bye at the door, he hugged me to his heart.

Shortly after that experience I wrote my first book, *Robes of Splendor*. I have never ceased writing since.

Then, here is one of the richest experiences of my whole life. In 1947, before we moved to California to make it our home, I was the preacher for the California Southern Baptist Assembly near Santa Cruz. B. B. McKinney, the beloved Baptist songwriter, led the music. We were assigned a cottage together.

I don't know what I did to influence his songwriting, but I know what I did to his heart. I managed, somehow, to crawl right into it. As we said our good-byes when the assembly was over, Ben McKinney, who was a big man physically as well as in every other way, grabbed me, swung me up in the air, and held me to himself with my feet entirely off the floor. He looked me in the eyes and said, "I love everybody because the Bible tells me to, but there are some people I sure don't like. I like you, though, even if you don't have sense enough to appreciate a good cigar." When B. B. McKinney was killed in that automobile accident, part of me died with him.

What costs less than a handshake or a hug? What, on the other hand, can pay one more?

Have you noticed that bumper sticker that says, "Have you hugged your kid today?"

Well, have you? If you do not have a kid of your own, why not hug someone else's? You could change the course of a child's life.

As for myself, I am glad that we are living in a time when artificial walls between the sexes are being penetrated and women and men can live together in society as human beings rather than just as male and female. I am not talking about the loathsome "Unisex" movement abroad in the land. I hate it. I simply mean that a man can—under certain circumstances—clasp a woman to his heart briefly, and vice versa, without raising eyebrows. He may even plant on her cheek a "holy kiss" and not be misunderstood by her or anyone else. Of course, I am talking about a natural, responsible, pure relationship—the *agape* of the New Testament.

Some things you and I as senior adults can never do again, either because of failing strength or limited opportunity. We cannot be quite as active as we once were. This hurts. There is something though that we can do better now than at any other time in our lives. We can show the greatest love and not have our motives questioned. We can put our arms around almost anybody with whom we have established fellowship and say, "I love you," and be believed. A handshake, a hug, or a kiss, can make the thirteenth chapter of 1 Corinthians come alive in someone's aching heart and troubled mind.

# 4
# Say Yes to New Adventures

I was never a Hell's Angel. I never tried to be an Evel Knievel. None of these characters were around when I was emerging from my teens, but I just loved to their last wheezing gasps the three motorcycles that I wore out more than a half-century ago. My friend Jimmy Walraven was the same kind of nut.

Jimmy and Rene Walraven have sung in the choir of the First Baptist Church in Albuquerque fifty-two years now. They try to look all dignified, standing up there in that choir loft. But I remember when they were not so dignified. Jimmy had a Harley Davidson motorcycle. I rode an Indian (motorcycle, that is). Jimmy would put Rene on the tandem seat of his machine, I would get Ina in the same place on mine and we'd ride off into the wild sand. And, may I point out this? Both girls rode sidesaddle. Their reputations would have suffered even more severely had they put on tight blue jeans and ridden straddle-legged.

Motorcycles in those days had no windscreens. You simply caught the bugs in your teeth. Of course it was hard to talk to anybody. Jimmy and I proposed to the girls while they were riding into the wind with us. We never heard what they said. No matter. We have all been married now these golden wedding years plus.

In addition to my pretty girlfriend who claimed all my waking thoughts, I had a grandmother who was a lively sort of character from the Ozarks, totally unafraid of man or beast. It is through her that I got my Cherokee blood, somewhat diluted with Irish corpuscles. Grandma Upton was visiting us for a month or two, and she was fascinated by my motorcycle. She kept pestering me to let her ride it. I am sure that she meant to drive it herself, but I would not consent to that at all. She might have wrecked it. Secondarily, she might have hurt herself. Her arguments persisted. If that girl I was running around with could ride it, she could too. Since Grandma was a visitor in our home, I was supposed to give her every consideration because of that, even over and above my filial relationship to her. But, then, there were limits to such considerations, I argued to myself, and in this Grandma Upton was off limits. I tried to warn her about how dangerous such an obstreperous iron bronc could be, especially to a *mature* woman. This merely hardened her insistence.

Next, I tried the aesthetic approach. "Whistler's mother never rode a motorcycle," I told her. "In every picture that you ever saw of that sweet little old lady, she was riding nothing more dangerous than a rocking chair."

"Keep that female, whoever she is, out of the argument!" yelled my grandma. "If you are afraid for me, I'll hang on to you like that girl does."

Oooh, goody, I thought, what fun that would be,

having my own grandma hugging me tight the way Ina did every time I made a port side turn. Aloud, I said, "No way!"

One day as I was trying to kick the motor into life and just as it caught, my grandmother, who had sneaked up behind me, thumped herself down *astride* the tandem. You won't believe this, but she looked exactly like Whistler's mother *from the neck up*. She wore a bonnet with the strings tied under her chin. The rest of her was stuffed down into an old pair of Dad's bib overalls, with the legs turned up about a foot.

"OK, your blood's on your own head," I yelled. "Hang on and lean with me on the turns."

We lived on Dartmouth, then the very last street in East Albuquerque (the house still stands). There was nothing between our house and Tijeras Canyon except a chicken ranch on the right side of the road. About even with our street, after a little jog, another dirt road went northeast toward Bear Canyon in the Sandias, about twelve miles away. One block from our house was the east terminal of the streetcar line, and, if I remember rightly, the pavement. Albuquerque was a sleepy little city of 20,000. Its citizenship was made up roughly, of 60 percent Spanish-speaking. Half the Anglo families had come West because of "lungers," as tuberculosis sufferers were called. There were relatively few automobiles.

I twisted my left wrist and throttled down until we had crossed East Central (Highway 66) and turned into the road toward Bear Canyon. I twisted my wrist to the right and gunned the motor. The tires dug into the gravel and Grandma tightened her hold around my middle. We were off—but not very far. We had not gone a half mile when I let my front wheel slip into a rut and had to correct too suddenly. Grandma's hold was broken. She claimed later that she just jumped off.

I braked to a stop, cut the motor, kicked the stand down, and ran back to where Grandma was just getting up. She shook my helping hands off and glared at me. "You did that on purpose," she said.

I argued that I had done no such thing, but she said, "I'll walk back home."

Again, I tried to argue. "But it's a half mile. Besides, you wouldn't want to be seen walking in that garb."

"I won't," she answered. Then, right in front of my startled eyes, she reached down and unbuttoned the metal buttons on each side of the overalls, reached up and unbuttoned the galluses, and let the overalls fall to the ground. As they did so, her long dress gradually dropped like the curtain on a stage. She stepped out of the little pile of overalls, walked up to my precious motorcycle, and kicked it just as hard as she could with her high buttoned shoe. Then, she turned, and without a glance at either me or my dad's overalls piled humbly by the side of the road, started walking back home.

I got my machine turned around, but I did not dare ride down the road toward where Grandma was walking. I had to sit in the saddle and watch her. Suddenly I started to laugh. Now that, I told myself, is a Grandma that any fellow could be proud of. Before that wild episode I had merely tolerated her. I had, of course, loved her, but it was just because I was expected to. Now, I found that I really liked her. We had had some fun together. Her bruised vanity would heal. My heart already had.

I am not suggesting that all grandmothers or grandfathers take to motorcycles. A couple of years ago I rode my last one. My bones are getting too brittle. There are, however, several motorcycle clubs over the land that are composed entirely of senior adults. One that I read about was in New York State. But motorcycling is not for all. Even my wife, years ago, lost her enthusiasm for such fast living. In fact, last summer, I had trouble getting her into my inflatable boat.

We were camped by a little lake on the Jicarilla-Apache Indian Reservation near its headquarters at Dulce, New Mexico. I laboriously pumped up the awkward-looking craft and put it afloat. My wife had never been in it. When I tried to coax her into it with me, she said, sarcastically, "I've got a bathtub at home."

I paddled out on the smooth waters of the tiny lake. As I stopped paddling and floated along, I saw a strange and beautiful sight. In the depths of the crystal-clear water, I saw masses of what looked like delicately woven green filigree curtains waving almost imperceptibly in the unseen current. Darting through these fragile tendrils were iridescent trout fingerlings, flashing their colors in the shimmering light. I called to Ina, "You don't know what you are missing." I tried to describe it all to her. The lure of the beautiful overcame her reluctance, and she consented to getting into the unstable little plastic raft. Soon we were sitting in the slow-moving cockleshell of a boat entranced by the aquatic display, seemingly spread out for our eyes alone. We would have missed it all had we not ventured out on the lake in our improbable boat.

Again, I am not hinting that all of us oldsters should climb into rubber boats and paddle out into the wild blue waves yonder. I do insist, however, that we can all enrich our remaining years with the zest of new adventures.

## We Can Leave the Past

Understand, I am not saying that we should forget the past. We neither could nor should. Our years that are gone hold many precious memories to enrich us, even to sustain us in the times of loneliness and uncertainty. They awaken within our hearts the spirit of thankfulness toward God for his goodness and mercy toward us. They are treasures which none can steal from us. We ought to cherish them.

There are lessons that we have learned, sometimes at the cost of much anguish. We can pass the answers to someone else who may listen to us and bypass that anguish to himself.

No, we should not forget the past, but we must not live totally within it. I think this is what Paul had in mind when he made his confession of ambition to his fellow church members in Philippi: "But this one thing I do, forgetting those things which are behind, and reaching forth to those things which are before, I press toward the mark for the prize of the high calling of God in Christ Jesus" (Phil. 3:13-14). The apostle was motivated by one high purpose: to please his Lord. He could not do this by just marking time. It could not be accomplished by his maintaining the status quo of his life. He had to break out of the confines of the past and move with certainty into the unknown of the future. We are invited to do the same.

In my early ministry, I heard a famous preacher talk from this text. He warned that we must forget our sorrows; we must forget our sufferings; we must forget our frustrations and failures; and, finally, we must forget our sins, since our heavenly Father has put them behind his own back.

I was moved by the tremendous power of the sermon, so much so that I have not forgotten it in four decades. But when the great preacher had finished speaking, I was aware of a vague disquiet in my heart. Something was missing from the roster of things we should forget. I know better now what it was. I know from my own experience as a reasonably successful man; I know it in the history of at least one church that I have pastored; I know it from the observation of many lives. What the preacher left out was that *we must forget our successes.*

This is particularly true of us who are senior adults. We can stultify our ambition to reach the high mark of Christ's favor by saying to ourselves, *But, look soul, what you have already done.* It is far easier to tread the stagnant waters of self-satisfaction than it is to swim against the moving current of useful action. We have reached a high plateau in life. We can sit down and rest awhile. As we rest, we can look backward down the trail up which we have climbed and face the sunset, or we can look ahead where the trail still climbs upward and face the sunrise. We are not yet through with the upward trail. There are still surprises around every turn. There are new delights for the heart; new feasts for the soul. There are challenges to the spirit. Remember old Caleb standing before Joshua and all the people on his eighty-fifth birthday. He flexed the muscles in his arm and waved it in the face of his commanding officer. "I am just as much man as I ever was, now give me that mountain!" He had been a good soldier and had helped to win many battles, but the war was not finished. There was still the unconquered mountain where the giants—the sons of Anak—barred the final possession of the Promised Land. Eighty-five-year-old Caleb said, "Let *me* at them!"

Simply put, we must break the binding chains of the past which prevent our spiritual progress. The thrust of Paul's statement is not the forgetting but the moving forward. We may not be able, like Caleb, to rout fierce giants from a mountaintop, or, like Paul, to honeycomb a Caesar's palace with believers, but we can refuse to retreat from life. We can help to rid our country of the giants of immorality, inequity, injustice, poverty, disease, and godlessness. Wherever we find him we can kill the giant of loneliness in another's heart. Each of us can reach for the goal toward which Paul had set himself. What was it? The Revised Standard Version of the Bible calls it "the upward call of God in Christ Jesus." What does that mean? It means that one blessed day, if we have done our best and have not given up the fight of faith, we can hear our Lord say to each of us, "Well done, thou good and faithful servant" (Matt. 25:21).

## Adventures in Friendship

In the preface to this book, which I hope you read (the preface to any book is usually an exercise in futility since most readers skip those pages), I mentioned my own deficiency in the matter of initially making friends. Friends do not just happen to come to me; I have to work to make them mine.

Many who will be reading these pages are better versed in the art of friendship than am I. Do not think that I am adopting an air of superiority—a know-it-all attitude. I write in the spirit of love and comradeship. I am conscious of what Paul also said in the verse that I quoted: "Not that I have already obtained this" (Phil. 3:12, RSV). I have not attained the complete art of friendship. I am still "reaching." I have learned some things, though, that have helped me.

When I retired from the pastorate four years ago, I was struggling with a deep-seated fear. I somehow felt that my only salvation would be to keep busy, mentally and physically. That, I succeeded in doing.

All my adult life I have combined preaching with writing. It was very easy for me to "change hats" from preacher to writer. I accepted a heavy writing load. In the four years of "supposed" retirement, I have written two full-length books, more than 100,000 words of Sunday School lessons, sixty 300-word devotionals, besides other articles for publication. In addition, I have been privileged to be a member of the staff of three Glorieta Chautauquas for senior adults. One week I served as Bible teacher and leader of the morning watch. The next year I served two weeks as pastor and preacher. Last summer I led a conference for pastors in two one-week sessions. Here I met some of the grandest people I have ever known. They came by bus and car from all over the country. They were happy, intelligent, friendly, and, above all, consecrated to God.

My wife and I had some recreation. We made one delightful trip with her Aunt Ruth the full length of the Baja California Peninsula, at Ruth's expense. We trailered coast to coast three times and once to New Mexico. On one trip we were gone seven months and on another, three. Every time I had to take along my typewriter and a folding typewriter stand—with a sundry collection of Bibles and reference books. Some of this book was written as I sat in the shade of a tall oak on the shore of beautiful Lake Eufaula in Alabama. That may account for some of its poor quality. I couldn't keep my eyes from wandering to a fisherman who had usurped my favorite spot. Every time he caught a fish, I had to run down and see what kind it was. I was able, also, to go to our cabin in the High Sierras every deer season and walk many miles in the wilderness, alone with God. In addition to all this chasing around, I managed to put a new roof on our house. (I built the house myself, in the first place.)

But, enough of the log of my activities. This has been the most rewarding part of my life, not merely because of my "busyness" but because, in keeping with the purpose of this book, I have deliberately set out to make friends for myself. I made some everywhere I went. I found it to be a most exciting adventure! That is why I want to share these ideas with you. I want to invite you to a bigger world than you have ever known before, no matter what your station in life or your varied experiences.

If you have reached this stage in life with a fullness of strength, I beg of you, do not dissipate it in useless inactivity. Reliable statistics show that you will retain neither your strength nor your life if you do so. If you have contemplated removing yourself from the social world, I hope to dissuade you from it. Down that path, too, lies death—this time to the spirit.

There is someone else, too, that I have in mind. It is the one who cannot leave home or hospital, the one who is bedridden. If you are one of these most precious souls, take heart. Let me illustrate again from my own life.

Because I did have energy and health, I let time become my master. I lived by deadlines and engagements—by calendar and clock. This caused me to lose, perhaps, more potential friends than I made. I have no secretary, thus I have to do my own typing, and as a typist, I am a good carpenter! Consequently, I have a stack of more than one hundred unanswered letters, some of them two years old. The letters have been so encouraging, so filled with expressions of love and interest that my heart was lifted toward heaven. But I did not make time to answer them.

Since I have been writing almost entirely for senior adults, most of the letters have come from them. *Many of the letters of encouragement have come from those who are bedridden.* I did find time to answer most of them.

Here is an adventure in friendship that can be practiced by loving souls who can no longer walk! Such messages may be written with faltering hands, but there is nothing faltering in their ringing testimony of faith. These are communications from the front lines of spiritual battle. How wonderful, how beautiful, how truly glorious such Christians are!

My wife's little mother died at the age of ninety-three. She had made her home with us for the last year of her life. Finally, near the end, we put her in the hospital for the last time. A few days later, Ina found a note in Mother's room. She read it and burst into uncontrollable tears. The letters were barely readable. Mother had Parkinson's disease which made her shake with palsy. Her poor hands were further crippled by arthritis. Yet, probably the last act of her life was to try to write a letter to her granddaughter, Valerie, who was expecting her first child. Mother, who had given birth to seven children, was trying to reassure the heart of a frightened girl. The last words for sure that she ever understood were whispered in her ear by my wife, "Val had her baby. It was a girl." Mother could not speak by that time, but a tear slowly trickled down her cheek.

Mother did not confine her love or her letter writing to members of her family. She was always trying to scrawl out a helpful little note to someone whom she barely knew. That is the kind of friendship that moves the world.

If you are one of those valiant souls who cannot leave your bed, I salute you. There are countless ones who need you. What is more, as you give out rays of sunshine from your heart, your own days grow brighter too.

Whoever you are, wherever you are, you can add a new dimension to your life: you can gather up a whole treasure trove of friends. This will not be a treasure locked deep within the walls of a bank, but jewels laid up for you in heaven. Listen to Malachi: "And they shall be mine, saith the Lord of hosts, in that day when I make up my jewels; and I shall spare them, as a man spareth his own son that serveth him" (Mal. 3:17). God's jewels—your jewels, for surely no one of us can point another to God without being, first, a friend.

## Then, On to the Adventure

As in anything else worthwhile, there are some do's and don'ts in climbing the trail toward friendship. This book expands on both, mostly by way of example. For this moment, though, let us examine others in capsulized form. We shall take the negative first.

(1) *Do not come on too strong.* Personally, I don't like a hail-fellow-well-met loudmouth who would slap my back into friendship instead of quietly beguiling me into it. He has the smell of insincerity about him. He would pull the wool over your eyes with one hand and pound you on the back with the other. You probably feel the same way. Such an individual is not looking for friends but for someone whom he can dominate.

Thankfully, if we are retired, we are spared much of that. We are no longer in any position to help boost someone else up the ladder of success by using our influence or position.

Neither (and it is hard to say this thankfully), do many of us have much money. Therefore, we cannot buy his insurance, his automobile, or the fancy house that he may be trying to sell.

Conversely, we are not trying to get ourselves boosted up any ladders either. We can be friends for friendship's sake. Furthermore, we have the time to seek and to cultivate suitable companions along life's way. We do not need to storm another's heart. We can knock quietly for entrance to it.

(2) *Do not try to buy friends*. Many lonely people do. Expensive greeting cards are sent with the expectation that like cards will be received in return. Gifts are extended in the wish that the recipient will be grateful enough to return at least a modicum of love.

Then, there is the more insidious way some persons try to buy another's return consideration: by excessive flattery. Flattery can fool no one unless that individual is pompous and conceited in the first place—an unlikely candidate for anybody's trust.

Now for some positive attitudes. Others will be developed in later chapters.

(1) *Refuse to be intimidated.* An Ozark Mountains farmer said it with a few words: "He puts his pants on one leg at a time, same as me."

Intimidation by others is a real and painful problem for many persons. It is at this point that so many faithful church members are misjudged. They find it exceedingly frightening to walk up to a stranger at church services and introduce themselves. They are not unfriendly; they are simply scared. If you are in this category, Barbara Walters has something to say that will help you (and me).

At the time Eugene McCarthy was running for president, Barbara Walters was working for NBC News. She interviewed the privacy-conscious wife of the candidate and asked about the sudden fame and attention that had been thrust upon her and how she bore it. Mrs. McCarthy replied that she had been nervous at first, but she cured herself one day by deciding, "I am the way I am; I look the way I look; I am my age." Marvelous advice!

Do not feel abashed in the presence of any other person on the face of this globe called the earth. In the sight of God, you are worth just as much as anyone else who lives.

Keep that in mind and you can walk right up to anybody and come right out with it—"Howdy." Or if that does not suit your temperament, say "How do you do?" You will find that it really did not hurt at all.

(2) *Sell yourself.* That sounds terrible, but hang on just a moment. I am not talking about money but about interpersonal relationships. You are somebody. Never forget that for a moment under any circumstances. Furthermore, you are worth knowing. In all likelihood, I have never seen you. There is something that I know about you, having never seen you. It is this: If I knew you, knew all about you (as the popular song suggests), and *if* I were a great writer, I could write the story of your life and turn that manuscript into a masterpiece.

Furthermore, the person who meets you needs to know you better. You have something to contribute to that person's life. If you do nothing more than show interest in him, as a unique individual, you have taken the long step toward friendship. That person has bought, through a deep and valid need, a part of you.

There are ways that you can sell yourself short. Some of them will be illustrated in story form in other chapters.

(3) *Be courteous*. Here are two people talking to each other. You know one, but you would like to know the other as well. Keep at a distance until their conversation is over. Does this sound like "cheeky" advice from me? Believe you me, many otherwise cultured individuals are careless at this point. I have received some frosty stares when, in my enthusiasm, I have forgotten.

(4) *Be able to accept rejection*. There will be some, for whatever reason, who will turn away from you, at first, or what is harder to bear, later on in your relationship. You *know* your heart, and you reach out toward another in the offer of unfeigned love and you are pushed away. I shall share a lot of personal secrets with you in this book. Now, let me confess: This has been the hardest burden I have ever had to bear in my relationship with others. I know well the feeling. You crawl back deep within yourself and you hammer at your own mind with the pathetic question, Why? You probably will never find the answer.

Deep love will always bring hurt. Sometimes the hurt is repairable; many times not. If we would have friends—loving, true, sweet friends—we must make up our minds to accept some agony in the process.

(5) *Give yourself*. Friendship is not an ego-stretcher. We do not seek it gainfully. Unless we are willing to give more than we receive, we had better forget the whole matter. Otherwise, we are entering the realm of the impossible.

Since the matter of giving of oneself will be expanded in narrative form in succeeding chapters, let us go on to other vital consideration.

## Go Where the People Are

Most of us, as active church members, have confined ourselves for the most part to our own special congregations. We have not had the time to learn how others live. We hardly know how other Christians conduct themselves.

I was invited to a senior adult banquet at a large Methodist church in our city. I was asked to give a review of my book on retirement, *No Rocking Chair for Me*. There was a large gathering of happy, well-adjusted oldsters. Among them I found the teacher of our class for older women. I walked over to her and said loudly enough for all around us to hear, "Maxine, what are you doing, hobnobbing with all these Methodists?" She said, laughingly, "I am a member of their club." I said, "Don't you ever let me catch you here again," and those near us laughed uproariously. They knew that I was joking. They did really ring the rafters when Maxine asked, "Why don't you join this club? You might learn something."

We all had a great time. Afterwards, I received a pretty little note from the president of the club. She invited me back. She said, "You are the only man I ever saw who could make a bunch of sourpuss Methodists laugh." I took that as she meant it—wholly in fun.

In almost any city there are clubs for senior citizens. They do all kinds of interesting and worthwhile things together. Have you ever been to one? Here is a sample of the activities (a few of them) of such a club in the city where I live. It is the club's own list:

| | |
|---|---|
| Serving of food | Outside entertainment |
| Quiet games | Educational programs |
| Active games | Business meetings |
| Parties | Visiting sick members |
| Excursions | Arts and crafts |
| Home talent | Community service |

Doesn't that all sound interesting? It does and is. The last chapter of this book is about *koinonia*—fellowship within one's church. That I consider to be the most important, but we need to go beyond it in fellowship. We need the broadening influence of other compatible groups without the church.

You probably will not have to look very far to find such a club of convivial, cheerful, helpful people near you. At least in such an atmosphere you can make new friends, whom you could never know without the exposure of yourself to them.

# 5
# "Have I Told You About My Operation?"

Of all the questions sure to put the listener into a state of catatonic, glassy-eyed mental sleepwalking, this one certainly takes the arsenic-sprinkled cake. It should head the lists of do's in any book on how to lose friends and alienate people. I am painfully aware of the fact that you could not care less about what was cut out, cut off, or sewn on to me or to almost anyone else, but, like everyone else, I will tell you about it just the same if you will listen. Please indulge me. After all, I have had just two operations in my whole life and I'll tell about only one of them. The reason I don't tell about the first is that it took place so long ago that I was in a room all to myself that cost $7.50 per day, including all the "fixins." So my memory is not too clear about it. But the real reason is that I was in a private room. I came out of that hospital as poor spiritually as when I went in. I had no one to talk to except the nurse who squirted painkilling poppy juice into my arm and the only thing I said to her was "ouch!"

But in my next hospital experience I met Bob. Before I tell you about him, let me fill you in with some bone cracking details.

It has been about a dozen years since I landed

in Community Hospital in the small mother lode town of Sonora, California. My ankle was broken in five places and I was practically in shock. The accident occurred at the 10,000 foot level just north of Sonora Pass in the High Sierras. Though I was then nearing sixty years of age, I had suddenly reverted to the recklessness of my youth. I was actually running down the mountain for no reason at all. It just felt good to be skipping along, dodging the huge boulders in my path, the cold wind whipping my face. Then, on the shale slope, I stepped on a rock that turned one way while I was going the other. There was a sickening snap, fully audible to me, and I crashed facedown on the rocks. After the wave of nausea had passed, I scooted along foot by foot some one hundred yards where I was stopped by a little stream. By this time I had attracted the attention of my wife who was picking flowers in the canyon below. To shorten this sad and painful and embarrassing tale, Ina and two friends of ours, Mickey and Alice Shannon, helped me to get to my car. Mickey drove us all down the winding Sonora Pass highway more than sixty miles to the hospital. It was late in the evening when we arrived and the ensuing operation lasted nine hours. Even today I wear five screws in my left ankle, and, thanks to God and to Dr. Paul Anspach, a renowned Seventh Day Adventist orthopedic surgeon, I can walk as well as ever.

After the long operation, during which I was given only local anesthetics, I was put to sleep and moved to my room. When I awoke later in the morning, the room was whirling crazily and I was nauseated. I looked over toward the other hospital bed and my eyes gradually focused on the face of a man of about thirty years of age. He spoke, cheerfully. "Hi," he said, "I'm Bob Wilmes."

I had not the slightest interest in who he was. Actually, I had very little interest in anything. I mumbled something and turned painfully on my side. Apart from the physical pain, I was mentally whipping myself. I had climbed some of the highest mountains in America without an accident. I had spent weeks alone in the wilderness areas of California, Arizona, and New Mexico. I was very careful at these times to assure that I never exposed myself unthinkingly to the possibilities of accident because there was no one to help me. I knew that mountain shale was never to be trusted. Yet, here I was, after a lifetime of boondocking, laid up like a tenderfoot. I was not really sore at my roommate—a man I had never seen before—but I was sore at *me*.

Later my fellow patient tried again. I had turned back toward him and was lying with open eyes.

"How did you get busted up?" he asked.

"I fell down a mountain."

"I wish I could say that," was the sour rejoinder. "I just fell off the porch of my cabin, barely two feet off the ground. Actually I fell from the second step. Me, who played left tackle for my high school football team. Fell down like a two-year-old. I only broke one ankle bone, but it hurt like I had broken half the bones in my body."

By this time I had recovered enough mental balance to act with a little more courtesy. I did not care to share intimacies with this acquaintance of an hour but at least I could try to be polite. I did not dream, in those first minutes of conversation, that Bob and I would become fast friends by the time we left the hospital.

From the beginning we were unlikely candidates for friendship. Bob is a staunch Roman Catholic; I am an ardent Southern Baptist. We were polarized in our religious thought but neither of us could escape the other. Neither of us could so much as leave his bed. At first I was a curiosity to Bob. He was not used to having a preacher around. What was more, we were imprisoned in a Seventh Day Adventist hospital. My nurses argued every time I asked for a cup of coffee as though I were calling for a quart of whiskey. Bob would not eat meat on Friday and the hospital would not serve bacon at any time. (What they called "bacon" was reclaimed half-soles from worn-out shoes, given a touch of redwood sawdust to make it more palatable. On this, at least, Bob and I were agreed.) There were other reasons that could have made friendship difficult. Bob is a Republican who voted for Kennedy. I am a Democrat who voted against him. Then there was the age barrier. Bob is just half my age.

Notwithstanding all this, Bob and I enjoyed each other immensely. The two subjects supposedly taboo in ordinary conversation—religion and politics—were discussed freely and at will. My new friend's questions about my religious faith showed perceptiveness and serious interest. While I thought that I knew all about Catholicism, Bob added a new dimension—his own personal testimony.

I liked to hunt; Bob hated it. I liked to fish; Bob hated that too. He liked to play golf and I told him that a full-grown man who would spend his time chasing a freckled faced little white ball all over a cow pasture was some kind of nut. Thereupon Bob would insist that a man who would get up before daylight, climb ten miles in rugged country after a buck, then almost kill himself dragging and carrying it out, only to give most of it away was, himself, nuttier than a fruit cake.

There was one idea on which we had no argument. Our little Irish nurse, Finnegan, was a sweetheart. We flirted with her unmercifully. Of course it was all proper. Bob had five children and I was a grandfather. Besides, Finnegan was quitting to get married to her own kind of man.

I never dreamed that anybody could enjoy a hospital stay so much. I was really reluctant to leave, dragging my hip-length cast behind me.

This is being written at Christmastime. Greeting cards from all over the country are pouring in. Dozens of them are addressed to "Dr. Dye." I am not a doctor. I hold no doctor's degree, earned, conferred, or bought. This is simply an ego patch that many strangers put on my name because of my prolific writing. These people are trying to compliment me. I can appreciate their motive but the card that has meant as much to me as any in the mail is a simple one with the usual little printed sentiment. I skimmed over that and my eyes dwelt with pleasure on the handwritten note at the bottom. "Hi, you old coot," it says, "have you busted any more legs lately?" It is signed, "Bob Wilmes."

This lightly-written little story may, or may not, have entertained you. That was not its main purpose. I learned a lesson that I needed badly to learn and I am trying to pass it on. I found a friend under painful circumstances, and he made me forget my pain. I would not have found my friend had I not unwrapped my own fuzzy blanket of selfishness and exposed my heart to him. Had I kept on concentrating on my own misery, I would have made things miserable for my fellow patient as well. I could have been so demanding that petite nurse Finnegan would have been glad to see me go. Instead, she seemed to be genuinely sorry when I gave her a tentative hug and told her good-bye. What is more, I would never have truly known my fine young companion on life's sometimes painful way—my friend Bob. That would have left a vacant place in my heart indeed. Then—I say it with due modesty, I hope—I would have robbed Bob of my own love, my moral support in his own times of pain, and of my personal religious testimony. The hospital door would have become the door of a jail instead of a doorway opening toward heaven.

You and I have walked life's pathways many years. We know the terrors of the trail. We know the hidden rocks over which the unwary can stumble to their moral and spiritual death. We have climbed a thousand mountains of sorrow, pain, frustration, failure, and seeming hopelessness. We have survived and somehow know that we are the better and the stronger because of our victories in those battles of the soul. We have climbed, like Moses on Mount Sinai, up into the "thick darkness [where God was]" (Deut. 4:11). There we have heard his voice with its message not for our ears alone, but for others through us. Perhaps we are, like Moses, climbing Mount Nebo, the last mountain of our life. The shades of night are falling over our trail. We *know,* where perhaps the younger ones can only guess, what the patriarch meant when he started that last climb. He said to his beloved followers: "The eternal God is thy refuge, and underneath are the everlasting arms" (Deut. 33:27).

This is our message, and it cannot be delivered effectively by some preacher standing above the clouds. His voice will sound too much like thunder. The sweetest word can only be whispered by a friend.

There is still a deeper consideration. There have been times when you and I have wandered from the trail. We have fallen into the abyss of sin. We have fallen only to be rescued by the Good Shepherd; to be lifted by his everlasting arms to safety and to love. This is the wondrous message that we share. Though I have spent half a century in the pulpit, my own experience has taught me that we can share the sweet old story best through friendship and not through sermonizing. The most good that I have ever done has been when I have taken the hand of another and have helped him back to the narrow Way.

One afternoon in the hospital, my friend Bob was greatly troubled. His serious face showed it and his halting words confirmed it. "I have something to confess to you," he said, "about a year ago I did something terribly wrong. I committed a moral sin."

I interrupted him. "I am not a priest," I said, "I am just a man no better than you are and perhaps not as good. I cannot say to you and mean it, 'I absolve thee.'" (I wanted to say, "and neither can any other man," but I did not do so.)

"I know that you are not a priest in the way I think of one. I simply must get this matter off my chest and into the open. I just want you to listen to me."

"Of course," I said gently.

Then my friend unburdened his heart. He told me about his temptation and his fall. His agony showed through every word. When he had told his story, he lay there quietly, his eyes searching my own.

I said, "Friend, I, too, have fallen. I, too, am a sinner." I told him who had helped me, who had said to me as only he could do so: "I forgive you."

Tranquility gradually came to the face of my young friend. Then he asked, wonderingly, "Why don't I feel this way after I confess to my priest?"

I lifted myself to one elbow and unlatched the sliding barricade on my bed. I swung my heavy long cast to the floor, stood up, and steadied myself against the dizziness. I hopped across to Bob's bedside and caught his hand. "Maybe, Bob, it is because when you go to the confessional, there is a wall between you and the priest" (and I wanted to say that it was more than a physical wall, but did not).

"He's right," said Nurse Finnegan, who had quietly appeared unnoticed in the room and was standing near the door. "I am a Christian, too, and I know he's right in what he says."

Bob shot a quick glance her way. Was this happy-go-lucky little Finnegan talking? he wondered.

The somewhat awkward situation was dissolved by her authoritative voice. "Now, you," she said, sternly, "get back on your bed and *stay* there." She took my arm and helped me back to my bed. When we turned our backs to him, I heard what sounded like a sniffle from Bob. Finnegan arranged the pillow under my head and said in her typical way, "Now I've seen everything. A Baptist, a Seventh Day Adventist, and a Catholic all agreeing on the same thing." She started to leave, then turned back to me. She leaned over and whispered in my ear, "Thank you for your testimony."

And I had not been talking to *her* at all.

My brother John and his wife, Pat, have just left our home for theirs in Orangevale, near Sacramento, California. This was their first trip since his release from the hospital. He had been rushed there after a diabetic illness which was critical. He was already suffering from severe heart problems for which he has been hospitalized twice, then this unsuspected diabetic condition struck him down.

I have given this explanation to show that my brother had enough problems of his own to turn his thoughts to himself and keep them there.

Instead, after the crisis had passed, he noticed a patient in the other bed. The man turned out to be a retired Air Force colonel. My brother, a much friendlier sort than I, tried to get acquainted with his fellow patient, but the old colonel would have none of it. His replies to all overtures were brusque to the point of discourtesy. John persisted. He told us, "I was challenged by his attitude and was determined to get the best of it."

John said that he was served a breakfast every morning that seemed to have been concocted by a dozen old hens. He said he was given fried eggs, poached eggs, soft-boiled eggs, and omelets "until I thought that I was turning into a featherless old chicken myself." He pled for a change in menu before he started "cackling." Finally he was promised that for breakfast the next morning he could have a "breakfast steak." Sure enough, the nurse's aide brought in a big covered plate and set it down on the bed table with a flourish. He eagerly lifted the aluminum lid and right in the middle of that big plate was the steak. He said, "You should have seen that steak! It was about three fourths of an inch thick, as a good steak ought to be, but it was about one inch square!" He called over to his room partner, "Look what they have done to me. I'm going to protest it. They brought me a plate that was already soiled. They left a little scrap of meat on it."

That got a laugh from the colonel, and the ice was broken, a little. But friendship started in quite a different way.

The Mexican cleaning girl was dusting the nightstand near John's bed and she noticed a Bible. He is a deacon in his church. Timidly, she asked him, "Perhaps, Señor, you could help me? I am new Christian for just about one month. Down the hall from here is a woman who may be dying. She thinks *es verdad*. She has ask me, 'Are you Christian?' I am say to her, 'Yes, but not for long time.' Then that poor woman, she ask me, 'Can you tell me if somewhere in the Bible it says that we can pray that we weel not die? Is eet wrong to pray for thees?' I am tell her that I do not know but I weel find out. Can you show me in that Bible something that weel help that poor lady?"

My brother asked for a few minutes of time and told the girl to stop by a little later. He took the Bible and prayed silently. He did not know exactly where to turn. Then, he told us wonderingly, for the miracle still held its glow, "I opened that Bible right where King Hezekiah was praying that God would let him live a little longer, and right there before my eyes was the answer. God did let Hezekiah live another fifteen years."

When the cleaning girl again stopped by, John handed her the Bible with the place marked. "Tell that woman to read where I have marked. Tell her that we have the same God that Hezekiah had, and she will understand."

Before long the maid was back and her black eyes were shining with excitement. Words poured from her lips in ecstasy. "Oh, that woman, she was so happy! First she cried, then she laughed. Then she caught my hand and pulled my face down to hers and kissed me." The girl handed John his Bible and said, "I hope you get well. Maybe you will," and she went tripping out to finish her cleaning work.

The Air Force colonel said, softly, "That was beautiful. I heard you tell the girl that you are a Baptist. I am, too, but I haven't been to church in years. I'm going to straighten up and fly right!"

My brother was dismissed first and he and his new friend exchanged phone numbers.

I assumed that the story was ended, but John said, "I didn't feel like going to church Sunday and about one o'clock my phone rang. The colonel was on the line and his voice crackled like static, 'How were church services this morning?'"

John had to admit that he had not gone. The receiver almost exploded in his ear. "Here I went to church in Sacramento like a good boy. Now, where in the devil were you this morning?"

My brother said, weakly, "Maybe you're right. The devil did get me, but I'll go to church tonight."

The apostle Paul had survived the shipwreck and was in Rome awaiting trial. He would long since have been dead, cast into the sea by the violent soldiers on the disintegrating ship, except he had made a friend. His conduct aboard the doomed vessel had won the heart of the centurion, who blocked the soldiers from murder.

Now Paul was in his hired house—probably paid for by his other friends in the church at Philippi. He was left a prisoner two long years while he awaited trial. During that time, he says that he was chained. It was probably during this period that he wrote to those Philippian friends and signed off his letter, "All the saints salute you, chiefly they that are of Caesar's household" (Phil. 4:22).

How did he make contact with those of the "imperial establishment"—as *The New English Bible* puts it? Did a jailer loose his bonds and go himself to tell the story to the palace guard? We know from Paul's own words that the "whole praetorian guard" was exposed to the gospel (Phil. 1:13, RSV). History has drawn a veil over the last days of Paul and the scholars argue endlessly about them. I have always been intrigued by Paul's expression, "the saints in Caesar's household" and Paul's link to them, also about who those "saints" were. Let me paint a little word picture.

The old man sat at a heavy table in an almost empty room. On the table were stacked sheets of papyrus. He wrote on one sheet and the quill made scratching noises as the old man traced large letters because he could hardly see.

Nearby, fastened to the older man with an iron chain, was a guard. The guard was young, burly, muscular. Another chain bound the guard to his prisoner, but this chain was unseen. It was a chain forged out of links of friendship. It was a chain forged by faith in the God who fashioned them both.

That chain did not exist at first. The guard was surly, resentful. He was on a hated assignment. He wanted to be on the outside, drinking wine with his carefree buddies. Instead, he was playing watchdog over an old prisoner—a Jewish troublemaker, a religious fanatic.

Before long the guard discovered that the little man by his side was no ordinary man. He was gentle, where he could have been hateful and angry. He was loving, where he could have been spiteful. He was considerate, where he could have been callous. He was one who cared for his fellowman, even when that man was his political and religious enemy.

One day, as the youthful guard watched the old man patiently writing at the crude desk, a vagrant thought passed through his mind. He pulled it back and examined it. Why did this man treat his known enemy so? The question would not go away. Determined to know the secret, he began to ask the old man questions. The answers made good sense. Communication led to friendship and friendship led to an even higher fellowship: the brotherhood of believers.

The young man said to himself, My buddies in the guard should know what I have found to be true: there is one God, not a pantheon of gods. There is a God who is holy and not corrupt in his own licentiousness. There is a God who rules through love and not through fear. That God came to earth and our own soldiers nailed him to a cross. He died for me as well as for the Jews.

I shall go back to the palace and tell the story of that Christ who was killed, his body put in a tomb with the door sealed with the imperial sign of Rome, but who, three days later, showed himself alive while the Roman soldiers slept like dead men.

You never read this in your Bible. You never read it anywhere else. Perhaps I have tampered with the Scripture where I had no right, but I have done no violence to the Bible by my imaginary reconstruction of Paul's prison experience. There is presumptive evidence that I could be right. Consider this:

Paul *did* reach another jailer. He *did* turn that jailer into a friend. He *did* witness to that jailer of the love and care of Jesus Christ. He *did* point him to the Lord and help his belief. He *did,* upon that jailer's profession of faith, baptize him. He *did* baptize the jailer's entire household in the Lord (Acts 16:23-34).

What I hope you will see is simply this: We can forget our unhappy circumstance; we can forget our pain; we can forget our frustration; we can forget our age; we can forget ourselves long enough to reach out to others and tell them the sweetest story ever told.

We are not in prison. We are not in chains. We may be old in years, as was Paul in these sundown days of his life, but, unlike him, we are *free.*

Then let us never bind ourselves with the chains of self-pity. Others hurt too.

# 6
# A Merry Heart Doeth Good

I could have headed this chapter "The Therapeutic Value of a Sense of Humor." I could have larded it with psychiatric double-talk and psychological gobbledygook and taken you on a mental roller coaster ride with occasional spinoffs into subconscious outer space, but I chose not to do so. I'd much rather compliment you by offering some occasionally hilarious suggestions and let you work out your own salvation if you need to.

More than threescore and ten years in this vale of tears have taught me that one of the most potent weapons in our arsenal against all manner of mental disorders and emotional hangups is a good laugh—preferably at ourselves. It would also help us to dissipate our own stuffiness and self-centeredness that keep us from having more friends if we laughed a lot more, even at life itself. And while I could lay some heavy mental stuff upon you from Freud, Pavlov, Jung, Perls, Berne, Rogers, Maslow, all of whom I have occasionally read with profit, I prefer to take another—and for me, a more authentic route—to get the message across.

There are some who insist that one is born with a sense of humor. If he has it, he inherited it from

Grandpa's genes, willy-nilly. Grandpa laughed when they tied a rope around his neck for stealing horses and cracked, "I hate neckties, and this is the worst I ever wore." Be that as it may, I believe that we can train ourselves to laugh. We can refuse to take ourselves too seriously.

I learned this lesson early in my ministry and every time I have remembered it I have gained serenity. Every time I have forgotten it I have wallowed in self-pity, torturing myself and everyone around me. The lesson did not come easily. My overblown ego had to be severely jolted first.

Once upon a time there was a town named Endee in New Mexico near the Texas border. The town is no more. I will not take responsibility for killing it, but I certainly shook it up. I also shook myself up.

During my college days, right after my ordination at the age of nineteen, I preached one Sunday in the little church at Endee. There is at least one other man besides me who remembers that sermon. I met him recently.

I have forgotten my exact text, but the sermon had to do with the kind of belief that brings salvation. I was turning loose such homiletic thunder that the shingles of the roof rattled, and the shaky walls quivered. "Do you know what belief is?" I shouted, "Belief is trust. It is more than intellectual acceptance," and I savored those words. Just then my eyes alighted on the communion table below the platform and the pulpit stand. It was not a choice piece of furniture but was roughly homemade out of unvarnished pine. I pointed to it. "I believe that table will hold me up. That is, I believe it with my mind.

But it is not enough just to believe that way. I must trust myself to it." Then I impulsively jumped from the platform to the top of the table to prove my theological point.

Things happened fast. All four legs of the table collapsed at once. I landed on my backside straddle-legged before the startled congregation, slid right into the feet of a woman on the front pew, and stopped. She kicked me! I was told afterwards that an old fellow who was sitting on the front pew across the aisle, had been sound asleep. He came wide awake, staring-eyed, jumped up and yelled, "What happened?" He was halfway down the aisle on his way out when someone caught him, sat him down, and whispering soothing words into his ear.

I finally regained my feet and stood there sheepishly until the laughter died down. I got back on the platform and tried to manage a faint grin. I don't remember what I said after that.

A retired Methodist pastor was in the congregation. He and his wife took me home for lunch. I was not hungry. "If you don't mind," I said, "I'll go take a nap." I wanted to be alone. I was afraid that I would cry. The grand old preacher led me back to a bedroom, told me to make myself at home, started to leave the room, and then turned back to me.

"Preaching is serious business," he said, "I know that. I gave my life to it. But there is something more than being a preacher. That's being a genuine human being. You got close to the people today, Son. Yes, you got powerful close to Sister Crockett on the front row," he chuckled. "She will never forget you, but she will forgive you. She may even come to like you, now."

He started to leave again, and again turned back. "By the way," he said, "I never thought that I would ever see a Baptist preacher give such an illustration of the good old Methodist doctrine called 'falling from grace.'"

His booming laughter dissolved my humiliation, and I found myself laughing with him.

"That's better," he said, "now let's go in there and help a poor chicken enter the ministry." I went obediently. My boyish appetite had returned.

But I had not yet learned my lesson.

At the age of twenty-seven, I became pastor of First Baptist Church in Las Cruces, New Mexico. The church was in dire trouble. It had suffered a splintering and the splinter group had formed another congregation. The beautiful brick building was being put up for sale to the highest bidder by the bond company which held the mortgage. I can see now, though I could not then, that probably the only human reason I was called as pastor was because a wiser, more experienced man would have turned it down. My salary to start was designated as "75 percent of the weekly offerings." The first month, the offering averaged thirteen dollars a week. Those were Depression times.

From the first, my pastorate in Las Cruces was singularly successful. I stayed ten years, saw the church out of debt, and its membership multiplied six times. But it might have been a different story had it not been for Mrs. Bowman, and she was not even a member of the church.

During my first six months things had gone so well that I became inordinately proud of myself. I was certain that I pastored my people with the wisdom of Solomon, preached to them with the fervor of Apollos, and served them with the dedication of Epaphroditus, the only man I ever heard of who actually did almost work himself to death in the church. I was certain that I, unlike the apostle Paul, had "already attained." That is, I was until Mrs. Bowman punctured my bubble of self-importance. The fact that she did not intend to do so is beside the point.

One afternoon the ladies of the church asked me to drive over to the First Christian Church and borrow some dishes for a banquet. In order for you to understand what happened, I'll explain that Las Cruces is the home of New Mexico State University. At twenty-seven, I looked like an undergraduate of that institution, especially in my shirt-sleeves without a tie.

Mrs. Bowman, the wife of the church custodian, filled my galvanized tub with dishes and then said to me, "I hear you've got a new pastor over there." I answered, "Yes." Then she asked me, "What do you think of him?" I was less than honest when I replied, jokingly, "Personally, I don't think much of him." She said, a little too quickly I thought, "Yeah, I been hearing there ain't much to him."

I stared at her a moment and saw that she was serious. Then I burst out laughing. I admitted to being the new pastor. She stammered, "Well, that's what I've heard." In the years that followed she could never look at me without laughing, and I laughed with her.

It is doubtful that anyone ever helped my ministry more than did Mrs. Bowman, who forced me to laugh at myself. I repeat it: *she made me laugh at myself.* She made me giggle my way off my sanctimonious pedestal.

Our ability to laugh makes us human. It makes us reachable. It can even make us understandable. It can—and will—increase our fellowship with our fellowmen.

We all like to be around people who laugh and who can make us laugh. My father's laugh, he said, was "like a donkey's bray." It did sound suspiciously like that, but it was infectious. When he laughed, everybody else laughed, then they laughed at their own laughing. He had many friends, both men and women. He also had grievous troubles but they never so obsessed him that he could not laugh.

Norma Zimmer is my favorite of all singers. She is beautiful in face, figure, mind, and soul. In her bestselling book, *Norma,* she recounts the story of her sordid, poverty-stricken childhood with an alcoholic mother and a sometimes brutal, drinking father. In the middle of the picture of hardship, disaster, frustration, and despair, she says:

"There was precious little laughter in our home. I have always loved to be surrounded by people who laugh freely. Perhaps because I enjoy it so much in others, I have developed a real humdinger of a laugh myself—not a tinkle as would befit a petite blonde singer. No, I have a high, hearty 'yuk yuk yuk' that sets others to laughing."

Who can say but that her ability to laugh was as much a factor in her success as was her rich musical talent? If you are addicted to the Lawrence Welk show, as I am, you know that this beautiful singer seems to have a sort of inward merriment. It touches all who come to know her, even briefly.

We senior adults need to laugh more. We need to do so for our own good. We need to do so for the sake of others. We need to show them that we have an inner peace, the kind that passes all human understanding, that we have claimed the promise of God: "And the peace of God, which passeth all understanding, shall keep your hearts and minds through Christ Jesus" (Phil. 4:7). This can be our greatest example, our most powerful testimony. Young people are watching us.

A young man leading the recreation segments during a conference for senior adults was so impressed by the rafters-ringing laughter of the participants that he said afterwards, "They make me know that their faith has endured, that it is real." Sour faces and tight lips would have had the opposite effect.

Do you think that because you walk with a cane that you have to be crippled in spirit. Elsewhere in this book I told about my little ninety-three-year-old mother-in-law who lived with us the last year of her life. Though most of the time she was wracked with pain, she was so filled with good humor that her very presence was a delight. The dreadful day came when she could not walk without assistance. We got a walker for her, but she snorted with disgust. She did consent, however, to walk with a cane.

One afternoon Mother was in our backyard walking on the lawn when she slipped and fell. She staggered at first and I saw her about to fall. I ran over to her but she went over backwards and sat down jarringly on the ground. As I bent over her to help her up, she managed a faint laugh. "I just got tired and decided to sit down," she said, smiling through her evident pain.

As I lifted her to her feet, I kidded her, "Well, you didn't sit there very long."

Again the smile, "I wasn't very tired," she answered, and her laugh almost made me cry.

When we had any kind of company, Mother, at our insistence, came in and was a part of the fellowship. I know, because they told me so, that many came to our home, not to see us so much as to see and be inspired by our gracious and cheerful little mother.

Mrs. Ethel Pope is a member of our church. She is ninety-four. Last Sunday morning I asked her how she felt. She cocked her head sideways, almost losing her little red hat in the process, and said, "I don't feel so good right now. You see, I had a terrible dream last night. I dreamed that I had got married again. To a handsome, black-haired young man who loved me so much he almost stopped my heart."

"Is that your dream—all of it?" I asked. "What's so terrible about that?"

"I woke up," she said.

"I'll tell you what," I said, "you find that guy and I'll marry him to you absolutely free."

"You'll do no such thing," she cried. "If he can't afford to pay the preacher, I won't have him. Do you think for one minute that I would marry such a bum and then have to support him all the rest of my life?" She shook her head so violently that this time she did dislodge that little red hat.

Wouldn't you like to know Mrs. Pope?

There is sound evidence that people who laugh

actually live longer. Grace Halsell in her book, *Los Viejos* (the Old Ones) tells about the year that she spent in Vilcabamba in the rugged mountains of Ecuador. She went down there to try to learn the secret of the long lives of the inhabitants who live longer than almost any other inhabitants of the earth, some as long as 132 years. She actually lived in the huts of Gabriel Erazo, Manuel Carpio, Gabriel Sanchez, Manuel Ramon, and Micaela Quezada, ages 132, 127, 113, 110, and 104, respectively. She found these citizens of the "Sacred Valley" to be among the poorest on the earth, with little to eat and no money at all. She concludes one chapter: "And most important, they are still working, and loving and lovable, and—what pleases me most of all—they spend a lot of their time *laughing*"(italics hers).

Perhaps at this point, you are saying about the author:

"What's the matter with this fellow? Doesn't he know that laughter and a sense of humor are not the same thing? He is talking about noise—even hyenas laugh."

You are right—except for the hyena. I never tried to tell a joke to one. If I left the impression that I believe humor, jokes, and laughter are synonymous, please forgive me. I have just finished reading a long book by a psychologist, and anthropologist, Ralph Piddington, called *The Psychology of Laughter*. I would have quoted from it but I could never understand what he was talking about. He quoted from writers, philosophers, psychologists all the way from Plato, the earliest theorist, to Kimmins *The Springs of Laughter*. All together, Piddington quotes from eighty-four sources. I came to the inescapable conclusion that not one of them knew what laughter is, in essence. So, there!

What I really mean, all technicalities aside, is that we should, and can, cultivate a sense of humor. We can learn not to take ourselves quite so seriously. We can even learn to laugh at life. We can communicate to our friends and neighbors, as well as our loved ones, our joy, our inner peace, and happiness.

Whatever laughter is, if we do more of it, we can go to our medicine shelves and throw away a lot of our pills—especially tranquilizers.

We may find that God knew what he was talking about when he inspired Solomon to write: "A merry heart doeth good like a medicine: but a broken spirit drieth the bones" (Prov. 17:22).

# 7
# How to Be Dull Without Even Trying

Years ago I wrote an amusing little story about one of our small grandsons. The piece had wide circulation and reader response was very gratifying. Because the anecdote is part of a larger truth, it is reprinted here.

Every grandparent reading these pages can identify with this story. Every such grandparent will, no doubt, agree with the conclusion which I drew. We would all be wrong.

The grandson is now grownup and married. He was not hanged by the neck until dead. He hasn't even been in jail. He is, in fact, a dedicated church member and sings in its large choir. He is a professional musician with a couple of college degrees to his credit. He plays and teaches classical guitar. He is a music composer and songwriter.

I once wanted to kill him.

The story is the plain, unvarnished truth except for the last sentence in it.

### Why God Made Grandsons

Our house is a total wreck. My wife is a total wreck. I, ditto. It is all because of Gary.

Now, Gary is one of those fearsome little creatures devised by the Lord apparently for one main reason: to keep a man humble. He is known, technically, as a grandson. He is also known to me as a freewheeling little demon.

Take last Saturday, for instance. It started as just another day. The sun came up in a perfectly clear sky. The air was brisk and stimulating. It was the kind of day when a man likes to work outdoors, and I decided to drive down to the church building and do a little work on the grounds. My work car is a jeep station wagon. It is fitted out with innerspring-mattressed bunks, stove, icebox, and all the other paraphernalia for camping. It is my pride and joy. It is also the pride and joy of every neighborhood kid. I have had to keep it locked at all times or it would disappear piece by piece.

I went over to the jeep and threw my tools in, climbed in, and started the motor. There was a sudden banging on the door. I looked out. Four-year-old Gary was whacking at the fender with a piece of one-inch board. "I wanta ride in the jeep!" he yelled, for all the world like cartoons I had seen of "Dennis the Menace."

I cut the motor and tried to reason. "I'm going down to the church to work. I'll be gone a long time. I won't have time to ride herd on the likes of you. Now, put that piece of board down, or I'll take it to the seat of your pants!"

"I wanta ride in the jeep," bawled my wife's grandson and punctuated the yell with another dent in my fender, whereupon I climbed out with blood in my eyes. Before I could carry out some particularly sinister intentions, my wife opened the front window and shouted so that all the neighbors in the block could hear. "Why don't you take him with you? He's been begging to ride in the jeep. Surely he won't hurt it, after all the rough country you have put it over!"

"But I am going to work. I can't take this screaming little maniac with me!"

After this time I saw the woman next door. She was looking at me with a smile. The man across the street stopped mowing his lawn and watched. Gary seemed to have plenty of reinforcements.

There seemed nothing to do but to give in, which I did as gracefully as I could. Gary's round face was split wide open with a smile that was nothing less than angelic. I felt a little mean.

We drove to the church without incident except once when I had to grab him to keep him from flying through the windshield when I applied my brakes in a traffic crisis.

Once at the church, things began to happen with the suddenness of a series of earthquakes. First, Gary spied a deacon hard at work in a three-foot-deep hole which he was concreting as a box for a storm drain. Gary bounded a rock off his shoulder. I beat the deacon to him and applied some child psychology from the palm of my hand. Next, my wife's grandson found a piece of candy which had been discarded by some child the Sunday before. The candy was covered with ants. By the time I got to him, Gary had it in his mouth, ants and all. I tried to shake it out of him, but only succeeded in partially dislocating his head. When he turned the outside hydrant on, I decided that I'd had it, as the saying goes. I pitched Gary into the jeep and took him home.

That night I sat in my favorite easy chair looking over my notes for the next day's efforts at preaching. Daughter Joyce was preparing Gary for bed, dressing him in a fuzzy sleep suit which made him look like a teddy bear. ("Deceptively sweet," I sneered into my sermon notes.)

"Kiss Granddaddy good night," said Joyce; and I found my lips smeared with a juicy kiss somewhat reminiscent of ants. Gary looked at me with a twinkle in his big, brown eyes. "Nightie, night," he said, as Joyce reached for him.

"I wanta pray," announced Gary.

"Of course, we'll pray," said Joyce. Her husband, Bob, joined her and they walked Gary back to the bedroom.

I laid my sermon notes aside, slipped back to the room, and cracked the door enough to see. Gary looked so tiny kneeling by his bed with Bob on one side and Joyce on the other. Then I heard him praying.

"God, bless Mommie. God bless Daddy. God bless Stevie (the baby brother); and, Oh yes, God, bless Granddaddy and the jeep."

I flinched at the postscript. When I tried to read my sermon notes I found them wet with tears.

Yes, God made grandsons to keep a man very, very humble.

My conclusion was wrong. God does not make mistakes. Neither does he fail. If he made grandsons just to make their grandparents humble, it didn't work. Did you ever see a humble grandpa where his grandson or granddaughter was concerned? And where is Grandma's humility where her grandchildren are involved?

All normal people love their grandchildren and are usually very proud of them. This is natural. The Southern Baptist Sunday School Board publishes an attractive and helpful magazine for senior adults called *Mature Living*. One of the most popular features of it is a section called "Grandparents' Brag Board." In a recent issue I noticed ten letters from proud grandparents covering a page and a half. This is good. We need to share such lovely experiences. On the other hand we don't need to bore each other to tears with our bragging about anything.

My wife fixed up a long, transparent credit card holder to receive the pictures of our thirteen grandchildren and two great-granddaughters (as of this writing). When some excessively proud grandmother begins, "Have I shown you a picture of my new grandchild?" my wife looks at the picture appreciatively then cuts the conversation short by taking the folder from her purse. She has a way of slinging it outward into the face of the other person so that it flashes through the light like a scimitar, reaching out three feet. That invariably upstages all other bragging and stops it dead.

Of course, one does not have to be a grandparent to be dull and boring. I know a woman who has the mangiest, the ugliest, the most moth-eaten cat that I have ever seen. She can talk about nothing else. I am not a cat-hater. I can take 'em or leave 'em. I can, though, think of many other topics of conversation more interesting than endless talk about the cleverness of a feline clown.

I do not believe that many things are more beautiful than an English pointer with one foot lifted, body straight from nose to rigid tail, holding on a pheasant cock hiding in the grass. He also is a thing of beauty as he works a field, always keeping about twenty yards out ahead of the gunner. But I have a friend whom I seldom visit because all that he can talk about is "Old Reggie." To hear him talk there was never another dog on the earth.

What about travel? I once sat at a table with six attractive gray-haired women who were unmarried—four were widows—and who seemed to have more than average incomes. They were active church members, and we were all attending a special conference. It soon developed in our conversation that all six of the ladies had been on trips to the lands of the Bible—two of them twice. They talked on and on, and on. I almost wore the seat of my pants out. Finally one of the women remembered me. "What did you think of such and such a hotel in Tel Aviv?" she asked me.

"I have never thought of it at all," I said.

"Didn't you stay there? Haven't you been to the Holy Land?"

"I've been to Texas," I told her.

"Be serious. You have traveled in Bible lands, haven't you?" When I shook my head, she reacted with unbelief, "How did you write all those books, those articles, and all that other stuff without ever going to Palestine?"

Twelve eyes looked at me for an answer. I felt like a kid with his hand caught in the cookie jar.

I never even intimated in anything that I wrote that I had ever been a member of the Baptist jet set with a Holy Land sticker on my suitcase. I can tell that story with safety because not one of those women will ever read anything again that I may write. I'm just not with it!

The point of all this is simply that we can run any good thing into the ground by talking it to death. We can repel those who would be our friends if they felt that they could be comfortable in our presence.

Lest you think that I am trying to whitewash myself, I must confess to one of the most detestable of all conversational habits. If I am with someone who stimulates me intellectually, I talk all the time. My long-suffering little wife says that I invariably try to dominate all conversation, that I butt in and never let the other person finish a sentence. Perhaps that really explains my antipathy toward the six Holy Land trippers. They would not let me tell about my fishing trip to the Sea of Cortez off the coast of Baja California. Now that was something else! One morning just at sunup I stood on a rock down by Bahia Los Angeles and cast a Wob-L-Rite Side-winder into the surf. Instantly . . . .

But, where was I when I interrupted myself? Oh, yes; I was saying, out of my own experience, we can put our tongues in freewheeling, many times not even enmeshed with thought, and drive our closest friends to utter distraction. We are not only discourteous to them but are cheating ourselves.

One of my good friends is Donald Ackland, of Nashville, Tennessee. Dr. Ackland is a native of England. He is a noted Bible scholar—a great teacher of God's Word. I have the highest admiration for him as a Christian, as an intellectual, and as a man. He teaches a men's Bible class in the Sunday School of the First Baptist Church in Nashville. I have sat in his class many times. Always, I learn something, primarily because I keep my mouth shut and listen.

On one of my trips to Nashville, Donald Ackland picked me up at the airport and took me some forty miles into the country where we were to be in a writers' conference. I started talking the minute I got into his car and did not catch my breath in the whole forty miles. I don't believe that I allowed him to say ten words on the entire trip. Donald Ackland is a gentleman like whom I wish I could be. We are still friends, mainly because of his Christian forbearance. I have thought many times what an opportunity I missed. I had this thoughtful man all to myself. I could have learned so much from him but I somehow got my tongue over my ears. (That may seem to be anatomically impossible to you, but I assure you, I can do it.)

So, not only can we be dull to others but also we can dull our own minds and thus impoverish ourselves when we talk all the time and never listen to what the other person has to say and share.

I may point out that the compulsive bragger and talker seldom recognizes himself as such. It is always the other person who is guilty. It is the other person who interrupts, who will not listen. It is the other fellow who is ignorant because he has a closed mind. He doesn't say much because he doesn't know anything to say. He has no opinions because he can't think straight.

Puck was right: "Lord, what fools these mortals be!" I am sure that in any lineup of Puck's such mortals, I would be right up front.

## Complainers

Any pastor standing at the front door of the church auditorium shaking hands with members of the congregation knows better than to use the familiar greeting to some, "How are you?" He knows that some individuals will delay the line ten minutes giving a clinical dissertation on their own particular ailments. To the woman, he says, "That's sure a pretty dress you have on." To the man he gives a similar ego stretcher, "I sure do like that striped tie." Thus, he shoos them by, if he is lucky.

I once helped a man to get a job as a receptionist for a large business firm. I was able to do this because the manager was a good friend of mine. One month later, the friend phoned me. "I had to let so-and-so go. Everyone who came by his desk tossed off the same customary greeting, 'How are you today?' and started by. The trouble was, no one could get by without a recitation of all of so-and-so's imaginary bellyaches. He made everybody else sick."

We all know persons like this, and we avoid them as much as possible. They are, in fact, sick. Theirs is an illness no medicine can cure. It is not lethal. They will not die physically from it, but it is deadly to social relationships. The sickness is called, "Self-Pity." We all suffer from it once in awhile.

The older we get the more we have to complain about and the more time we have to do it. We do, in reality, have more aches and pains. Some of us hurt a little all of the time and a great deal once in awhile. That is the price we have to pay for living in a body that is fast wearing out.

My hobby, since childhood, has been shooting. I was once a member of an international rifle and pistol team. I own a prized revolver, a .38 Special with which I won some matches in the long ago. I load my own ammunition for it.

One month ago I took my revolver and shooting case out on the range to do a little paper punching. At fifty yards I never hit the X ring once. One of the secrets of good handgun shooting is to squeeze the shot off by an imperceptible movement of the finger on the trigger. I could no longer do that.

When I returned home, I was disgusted with myself and took it out on my wife. "I'll have to quit shooting," I stormed. "Arthritis has so stiffened my trigger finger that I can't control the shot . . ." on and on, *ad infinitum, ad nauseum*.

She said, weakly, "I'm sorry, dear."

One afternoon, last week, two young women from the church called on us. We have known them and have loved them almost as our daughters for many years. They sat on the lounge facing my wife and me in our easy chairs.

Ina was knitting an afghan of orlon yarn. It was almost finished. The girls were ecstatic over its beauty. The afghan is five feet wide by six feet long. There are five panels, two shades each of brown, and a center one of gold. The whole thing is bordered by gold crochet. It takes my little wife a whole year of spare time to fashion this covering. This is the second one that she has made. The first went to our oldest daughter, this is for the second oldest, and two more are scheduled, one for daughter number 3 and the last for our son's wife, daughter number 4. No two are alike.

Our visitors chimed, "That is a lot of work!"

Ina's flashing needles stopped for a moment. "Yes, it is," she said. "I am trying to get them all finished before arthritis so cripples my hands that I can't do it." This was said matter-of-factly, and the quiet words were covered by a sweet smile. I looked over at her hands, which were still for a moment. I can't remember that she had ever mentioned her arthritis to me. I glanced away with eyes suddenly filled with tears. Had there been no visitors present, I would have moved over and covered her hands with kisses. To me, they are the most beautiful hands in the world.

I had just one finger that had grown stiff and had crippled my childish play. Ina had ten pain-filled fingers that could not cripple her love.

Is not that always the way it is? We hurt a little and are tempted to make a big thing of it. We do not look far, though, before we find someone else—perhaps right by our side—who hurts so much more and hardly mentions it. Everybody with any sensitivity loves and is inspired by such a valiant soul.

## A Listening Heart

If it is true that we can drive others from us by our incessant bragging and complaining, it is no less true that we can draw others to us by sympathetic attention to what they say about their real problems. Listening is a virtue that cannot be overrated. We can only cultivate it by getting away from our own egocentricity (self-centeredness).

Do you truly want to be loved? Love is like happiness in that one cannot go looking for it and find it. Going a little deeper into the argument: happiness is the by-product of love and both are possible only when we forget ourselves. When we love others, we are loved in return. Paradoxically, when we forget ourselves in such love, we find our true selves. Do you remember that old song we used to sing? "You're Nobody Till Somebody Loves You"? Those words are eternally true.

Now, consider this. All around us are lonely, frightened, hurting souls. There is no one to whom they can talk, no one who cares enough to listen. Some are young people who feel rejected by parents or society or both. They need friends. You can be such a friend. Do not feel intimidated by them. That so-called "generation gap" is a myth. If you can listen without being judgmental, if you can love without hypocrisy, you can succeed far more often than you fail in gaining the friendship of the young. In the final analysis, you are "somebody" when you live in the heart of someone else.

# 8
# Watch Yourself Go By

> As for looks I was never a star
> There are folks better looking by far,
> My face, I don't mind it,
> You see, I'm behind it;
> The folks out in front get the jar.

I have collected that little bit of doggerel verse out of my own memory. I can remember my father quoting it in a speech that he made when I was a little boy. He thought that Woodrow Wilson was the author, or, maybe Abraham Lincoln, neither of whom was a very handsome man. Be that as it may, no matter how we may try to sidestep it, there comes a time when we have to take a look at ourselves—and we should.

The Bible tells about a fellow who looked at his face in the mirror, straightway turned away, and forgot what he looked like. Was that a defense mechanism against shock—contrived forgetfulness? James does not say.

In my time I have owned every major brand of electric razor produced so far. The last one was so heavily advertised that I plunked down forty inflated dollars for it. I could shave with the blasted thing all day long and my whiskers would grow faster than I could cut them off. There is an advantage in the electric shaver which I fervently desire. One does not have to look at one's self when one shaves one's face. That is good English. Translated into workable wordage it means for me that I don't have to look at my silly face when I scrape off my beard. Thereby I escape shock. That is why I bought so many electric razors.

I also own a beautiful old straight-edged razor made in Germany nearly one hundred years ago. That will shave a baboon. But one has to look at one's face in the process or else one will cut one's long nose off.

Simone de Beauvoir tells about a conversation between two great men about "that frightful thing, growing old." Paul Valery, a wise man, a master thinker and writer, confessed to his friend Leautaud that he did not want to talk about growing old. He said, "I never look at myself in a mirror, except when I shave." A prominent psychologist says that he has treated several neurotics who suffered this phobia about mirrors because they did not accept their bodies. Paul Valery was not neurotic. He was a scholarly man, keen-minded, alert, and friendly. He was willing and able to examine himself, and he had to admit that he could not bear to look his old age in the face.

So, I am not alone. I stand somewhere between the nameless neurotic and the master thinker. I, too, dislike looking into the mirror and staring into the face of an old man. But I do it unless I am in the woods alone. Every day I shave that same old man. If I speak twice in public that day, I shave the old man twice. The older I get, the more I want to salvage any good looks that I may once have possessed. I do not wish to offend others. I want to be accepted by them. I would very much like to pull them toward me, not drive them away. You may counter, "But beards are accepted by almost everybody today." That may be true, but a man with heavy whiskers simply looks dirty with a two-day's beard. He looks as though he needs a bar of Lava soap.

It would be helpful to any of us if the plaintive plea of Robert Burns could be answered: "O wad some power the giftie/gie us/To see oursels as others see us!"

We can never quite do that, physically or otherwise, but we can do our best to see ourselves as a stranger sees us who may share a little walk with us.

For more than fifty years my wife has had to help me dress myself. Not that I am crippled. I have everything bodily that I started life with. Along the way I have shed a few teeth and a lot of my hair, but I didn't have any teeth when I was born and had about the same amount of hair that I've wound up with, except now it is longer. Anyway, who needs teeth to pull on his pants?

No; I am not crippled physically. The reason my wife has helped me to dress is because I am partially color blind. Again, I do not stand alone. Researchers say that 25 percent of all men are color blind red to green. That is why modern hunting jackets are blaze orange; all hunters can identify that color and thus may not shoot antlerless men. Women seldom have the problem of color blindness. Only one in twenty-five is afflicted in this manner.

All my adult life, as a preacher, I have walked in the public eye. I have never been known for my sartorial perfection. On a scale of one to ten of America's best-dressed men, I could not make it past zero. If I ever was presentable in a public place, it was because of my long-suffering wife.

I would go off to a revival meeting with a couple of suitcases full of my clothes. In my hotel room, or wherever, I would open the suitcases. I would take out the first shirt. In the pocket I would find a note. The note would say, "Wear this with your brown suit." Then the brown suit would have in its breast pocket a tie folded carefully (she dared not pack the tie separately). I knew to wear that tie with that suit. Ditto for my other suit. (I had two suits then, you understand; I was not retired.)

Once I was laying out my wardrobe on such a trip and I found a note in my white shirt. I muttered to myself, "That fool girl ought to give me some credit. She ought to know that I can wear my white shirt with anything." I took out the note and read, "I love you." It was signed, "Niney"—my pet name for her. That was probably forty years ago. I carried that note in my billfold until I wore it out.

One Sunday, a few weeks before I retired as pastor, my wife made me change my tie two times because it did not match the seat of my pants or for some other ridiculous reason. We started off to church. I was the most perfectly color coordinated man in town. Suddenly I began to laugh. My wife asked, "What's so funny?" I said, "My tie matches my shirt, my shirt matches my suit, my socks match my shoes, my shoes match my suit, my belt matches my pants, but," I said gleefully, "I've got on purple shorts!"

"Where did you get them?" yelled my wife.

"I bought them because they are pretty. I'm wearing them because I want to . . . ."

"Watch out! There's a red light," cried my wife.

"I can tell a red traffic light," I said, stiffly, as I braked to a stop, "the red light is always on the bottom."

My piety may have suffered that morning, but my ego did not.

What I am saying is, I once looked presentable because my wife made me. Now I try to make myself presentable in self-defense against the world.

I want my wife to look her best too. The other morning I just happened to see a cosmetic jar on her dressing table. She had not put it away and I got a glimpse of the price on the lid. Do you fellows have any idea what that perfumed lard costs? That small jar was marked ten dollars and fifty cent—and that was without tax! Why, that would buy me enough shotgun shells for a whole hunting season! What is more, I found out that the same size jar of the goo could cost up to twenty-five dollars, depending upon what cosmetological princess had her name pasted on it.

That's not all. Every night I get into bed and wait up to fifteen minutes while she smears that smelly stuff on her face. She does that in the dark. She puts the stuff on, then she rubs it in, then she rubs the rest of it off. I don't know exactly what all it is expected to accomplish, but I have long since decided that if it will keep her pretty—and she is prettier than most—it is quite all right with me.

# Look Your Best

In my forty-six years as pastor, I, as any pastor does, have had to counsel with many married couples whose differences had reached the stage of incompatibility—grounds for divorce in any state where I have lived. In all too many instances the wife had simply let her physical appearance go. (After all, she had caught her man; why keep on baiting the hook?) She neglected her hair—sometimes even went to bed with it wrapped up in metal curlers as though she were wired up for a trip to the moon. She neglected her face, her body, and sometimes her manners. The husband lolled about the house when he was not working, with scratchy whiskers on his face, and other evidences of a noncaring attitude. Eventually all physical attraction for each other was lost.

Then, all too often, either husband or wife became the prey of a worldly-wise member of the opposite sex who set up what the young people call "vibes"—well, you know the rest of the story. Besides, it is outside the purpose of this book except to provide illustration.

Marriage problems aside, too many persons who reach the age of retirement say to themselves, "I am a nobody now. I have been discarded by society, so why should I care any longer how I look? I'll act the way I want to; I'll dress to suit myself." The man's first defiance of the outside world may be to appear in public with unshined shoes. (After all, if you can show me a man who likes to shine his shoes, I'll show you a woman who likes to wash dishes.)

From that stance he carelessly drifts into other unsocial attitudes. On the other hand, he may try to imitate the flamboyance of youth or even its slovenness. I tried that, once!

I started to the hardware store one day and kissed my wife good-bye, as I always do when I leave on any trip, short or long. After returning my kiss, she reached up and buttoned my leisure pullover shirt that I had left open too far. "If a man's going to show the mass of hair on his chest, it ought not be gray." Wham!

What shall I say to my women readers? If I had reasonable intelligence, I would say nothing at all. Not having such intelligence, but having enough integrity to try to make this book what it ought to be, I'll venture to say this and run like the dickens. Dress neatly, but for your own sake, dress in keeping with your age.

Did you notice that pretty teen-age girl tripping by you yesterday on the sidewalk? She had on a tank top with its tail pulled out and flapping in the breeze. She wore what was left of a pair of faded blue jeans, frayed on the bottom, and patched in four places. She could, and did, get by with it. Her body was well-proportioned in the symmetry of youth. Her step was light as a fawn's and she vibrated with the joyous vitality of adolescent life. She would have been strikingly pretty dressed in a gunnysack. 'Nuff said, except for one more thing. The attractive blue jean wearer was pretty, but she was not beautiful. Some day, in all likelihood she will be, but not yet. The old cliché is right: Beauty is more than skin deep. Beauty comes from within the soul, and flows outward. The greatest beauty that any woman can have is that which comes from a glowing character forged in the fiery crucible of time. So, dear lady friend, you have the undeniable advantage; do not throw it away through carelessness. The most beautiful creature that God ever made is a godly woman with his image stamped forever upon her soul. Let the world always see you that way. It desperately needs to do so. Aside from Christ, you are the greatest redemption that it has.

Last Sunday morning I was standing in the foyer of our church auditorium looking out. Through the big double doors, I saw a little woman coming up the sidewalk. I knew that she had walked from the apartment where she lived two blocks away. As she turned into the walkway leading up to the building, I noticed that her face was tired, drawn-looking. Her steps were slow, labored. As she drew nearer, I saw that her nicely tailored dress was royal blue, polyester knit. Tiny red flowers danced on the folds of the dress. She wore matching blue earrings and necklace. Her white hair was waved and looked like snow blown into ripples by the wind. Her black patent pumps complemented a black purse. Over her arm she carried a lacy white knitted stole. She is one of my favorite people. She is ninety-three years old.

As she looked up and saw me, she gave me a pretty smile. She wears no glasses and tiny smile wrinkles are permanently etched around her eyes. I gave her a great big hug. In a moment she said, the smile broadening, "If you will please turn me loose, I'd like to go to church."

The dear old saint marched right in, her head held even a little higher.

To add a note to the valiancy of this little great-grandmother, to my certain knowledge, she has little more than a bare subsistence income. I want to make that clear because already someone may be saying, "What's the matter with that smart aleck? Doesn't he know that clothes cost money? How can I get all dressed up on what is left of my Social Security check?"

I am not talking of trying to keep up with the latest fashions. My own lapels are still too narrow and my ties, the same, and I am still wearing the dress shoes that I was wearing when I retired four years ago, but I do try to keep them polished. I know as well as you do that it is hard to give fifteen dollars for a dollar-and-a-half shirt.

I had a pastor friend who served a small church in this community where I live. Mac was the nattiest dresser that I ever knew in the pulpit or out. One day I said, "Mac, how on earth do you manage to dress so nicely? I know that you can't possibly make too much money." (I could say that because of years of friendship.) My friend laughed and said, "You have to know your tailor."

One day my wife and I were driving along a back street of our city when she suddenly shrieked, "There's a Thrift Store! Pull in there." She has this thing about stringing beads. She can never pass up a rummage sale, a Goodwill Store, or a Salvation Army Thrift Shop. She searches for strings of glass beads, then restrings them. She has one narrow floor to ceiling cabinet in the hallway of our home filled top to bottom with gorgeous necklaces of beads. She has another wall cabinet in the bedroom, filled with the same. Once in awhile she sells a string to give her more operating capital, but, mostly, she gives them to the many girls and women of our family.

On this particular day, while she was pursuing her hobby, I started back to look at the rows of secondhand books. It was then that I saw my friend, Mac. He was trying on the coat of an expensive looking suit. He saw me at the same time and motioned me to him. "Now, you know," he said, "just look at this suit. Twenty bucks. Good as new."

Mac is gone now. Anyway, I changed his name so as not to embarrass him and give away his secret. The only point is: No matter how we manage to do it, in these later years, particularly, we should try to look our very best.

### Smile, You Are On Candid Camera

I am not going to propose that any one of us go out in public wearing only a smile. There is probably no longer any law against it, with all this permissiveness, but I do believe that we should wear something more. On the other hand, if you are all dressed up like a Sears Roebuck clothing ad, you will still push others away from you with a perpetual frown.

I am not suggesting that you run around looking like a Cheshire cat with a grin as false as a model's eyelashes. After all, that poor old English cat can't help looking silly. We can. A phony smile is as easy to spot as is a Band-Aid on one's nose. It cannot even fool a child. (Come to think of it, not many of our hypocrisies can.) Neither can it persuade any of our peers that we are either happy or friendly or are even to be trusted.

I mean, simply, that we can look pleasant and cheerful when we are out with others. Of course, nothing that is being said here is profound. It is not even informational. It is simply a reminder both to the writer and the reader that first impressions are usually lasting.

Have you ever noticed how an otherwise ordinary human face can instantly be turned into one of unforgettable charm? We all have. The secret is a happy smile. We instinctively want to know such a person better.

On a recent trip I spent three hours between planes at the huge Dallas-Fort Worth airport. That asphalt jungle seems to sprawl over as many acres as does the King Ranch. If you change airlines you have to go down to the lower level in an elevator to the Air Trans station. Then you discover that in order to board the commuter train you have to produce a quarter for the turnstile money box. Since you don't have a quarter, and there is no money changer, you go back up the elevator to the upper floor again, walk a mile or two until you find a newsstand. Then, if you are a little timid, you flash a dollar bill and fork over twenty cents of it for a nickel roll of mints because you are afraid that haggard-looking woman at the cash register will bite you if you don't. You wouldn't dare ask her outright to change your big money into little. Then you dash back to the elevator, go back down to the turnstile, drop your quarter into the box, and get into that side of the area.

You now face a glass wall with two sets of sliding doors. One set allows access to the front part of the train and the other to the rear. But you can't get on the train because it isn't there. Besides, the first train that comes by won't be yours, anyway. You watch a board which lights up slots for different airlines. Each train runs by coded colors. If you are flying Braniff, for instance, an orange color will show in the slot beside the name of the airline, and the same color will show near the front of the two-section train. (I may be wrong about the color, since I am writing from memory, but the procedure is the same.) Once on the train, a beeping sound alerts you for your airline concourse.

Has reading about all that made you as tired as it has me in writing it? Then on with the story, skipping such details. I just wanted you to see why everybody you will see in the Dallas-Fort Worth Airport is crazy. If he is not when he arrives, he is by the time he departs. That's why I could sit three hours in the waiting room while hundreds passed by and never see a single smile.

Well, now, back to the commuter train. I had managed to get on the right train. Just before the automatic doors closed, a blond, fifteen-year-old girl flew through them and landed on the seat beside me. She settled back with a rasping sigh. We were the only passengers. When the train shuddered and finally got moving, I turned to the girl beside me. She looked forlorn and distressed. I smiled at her and said, "I hope you are a good engineer. This train doesn't have one." She looked startled, then smiled back at me with quivering lips. "I've got to get to Albuquerque today," she said, "and I was afraid that I had missed my plane."

We boarded the Texas International plane together. I found my assigned seat and she went farther back to hers.

I had settled down to my *Reader's Digest* when I

felt a light touch on my shoulder. I looked up into the face of the fifteen-year-old girl. Her face wore a look of acute distress and there was the hint of tears in her lovely eyes.

"May I sit with you? The stewardess gave me permission." After she had settled herself, my young friend said these revealing words to me. "I need to talk with someone. You have such a kind face that I felt that I could talk with you." (She never said what "kind" of face I had, and I did not ask.)

The miserable little seat companion poured out her story to me in a tumble of words. She had run away from home with a boy who had deserted her in Dallas. She had no money when he left her. In desperation, she phoned her parents in the New Mexico city and they had wired her the money to come back.

"Oh, I don't see how I can face them!" she cried.

I reached over and patted her hand, reassuringly. "Don't worry. It will be all right. If you want me to, I'll help you face them. I am a minister. The only reason I live is to help people like you if I can."

Her relief was touching. We talked all the way to Albuquerque. I told her about my Christ and led her to accept him. I told her that she would find a warm welcome in the First Baptist Church in Albuquerque which is across the street from her high school. I told her that, although I had not lived in Albuquerque for more than thirty years, I knew how she would be treated by the pastor and members of that church. She warmed even more to me when I told her that I was a graduate of Albuquerque High, class of '25.

When we landed in Albuquerque, I lingered discreetly behind and watched my pretty seatmate enveloped in the arms of her father and mother, both at the same time. As I passed by, she smiled over her father's shoulder and her tears were like luminescent pearls dropping down upon his coat. She waved with her free hand, and I went on my way. Her parents never knew that I even existed—and that's the way it should have been.

You may never be caught "in the act of being yourself" by the lens of Allen Funt's candid camera, but you will be caught in the eyes and the heart of some would-be friend if you radiate your own serenity and happiness through a smile.

# 9
# Wear Your Age Proudly

About a dozen years ago, when I was a youthful sixty, I fell in love with a beautiful girl. I also fell out of love with her in about thirty seconds—the shortest love affair on record.

The young lady had just moved next door to me. I saw her out in her front yard and ambled over to get acquainted. She welcomed me with a wide smile, sparkling with flashing white teeth. She had dancing blue eyes—the kind that would make any fellow's heart turn a cartwheel or two. Blond hair curled around her oval face and, backlighted by the late afternoon sun, was a halo around her head. She looked like an angel straight from behind the variegated walls of heaven. She was every inch a regal princess. The trouble was, she was barely thirty-six inches tall.

I knelt down and said, in my best grandfatherly way, "Hi, Sweetheart."

The dancing eyes stopped their dancing. They bored steadily into mine. The dazzling smile faded like dew before the ten o'clock sun. "You are old!" she said, in an unangelic voice.

Behind me I heard a stern voice. The mother had come from the backyard to investigate the strange man in her yard. She evidently was reassured as she recognized me as the man she had glimpsed next door. "Shame on you, Emily, you shouldn't say things like that to the nice man."

I was already getting stiffly to my feet. I turned to introduce myself to the little one's mother. The new neighbor graciously acknowledged the introduction, then added, "I am sorry for what my Emily said to you. I know that you must be terribly offended at her calling you 'old.' It certainly would have offended me."

I looked at my new acquaintance. I judged her to be about twenty-five years old. If sassy little Emily grew up to be as pretty as her mother, she would be a knockout, I thought. Aloud, I said, summoning all the warmth that I could into my own smile, "It would have offended me, too, at your age. But, after all, Emily is right. I *am* pretty old. Every day I find this out in a different way."

Emily and her mother have long since moved away and have passed out of my life completely except for the memory. Once in awhile that brief encounter in Emily's front yard comes back to mind. I hear the scornful voice of a child, little more than a baby, "You are old." Then the shock in the mother's voice comes through the years to haunt me: "Shame on you, Emily . . ." and to me, "I know you must be terribly offended at her calling you old."

Of course, what the child said held no significance whatsoever except as the statement of an obvious fact. On the other hand, what the mother said so solicitously, enwraps an almost universal societal concept: Those who have lived to retirement age and beyond ought to live apologetically if they live at all. To this, after profound consideration and scholarly research, I answer, learnedly, "Baloney!"

I was not ashamed to admit that I was sixty. Neither do I flinch, assume a woeful mask, and, pressured into a corner from which there is no escape, plead guilty to being seventy-two as though it were a capital offense. Why should I? What crime have I committed? Did I embezzle those years from the lockbox of time and rob someone else of them? Did I, simply by living beyond my supposed allotted time, make a lewd prostitute out of Mother Nature? Have I kicked all young people in their collective face? Have I committed fraud against the government and swindled the taxpayers by drawing Social Security for which my employers and I paid our legal share?

I refuse to be intimidated by society just because I did not get killed on my motorcycle fifty-five years ago and am lucky enough not to have died from an overdose of ingrown toenails.

I do not intend to wear my age as a chip on my shoulder, double-dog daring anybody to knock it off. I am not going to parade it. Neither will I try to hide it. I shall wear it proudly, as a God-given extension of myself. How about you, dear friend?

## We Must Admit Our Age

Do you really feel older—on the inside of you, I mean? Your eyes look out on the world you have always known. The Milky Way still girdles the midnight sky with its 100,000 million stars flickering like diamond dust. The pointer stars in the Big Dipper still point to Polaris, the North Star, as they have done all your life—and for ages before. The sun still comes out in the morning like "a bridegroom coming out of his chamber, and rejoiceth as a strong man to run a race" (Ps. 19:5). Sunsets are as beautiful as ever, flowers are just as sweet and are clothed with the same fragile gowns of sun-kissed glory; the trees grow tall; the mocking bird trills, and the meadow lark sings in the early dawning. Green grass carpets the rolling hills, the raindrops fall as they always did, and the rivers run into the seas.

Your heart leaps up as it always has when beauty fills your soul.

You still have dreams. You dream of a better world where all people can live together in peace and "they shall beat their swords into plowshares, and their spears into pruning-hooks: nation shall not lift up sword against nation, neither shall they learn war anymore" (Isa. 2:4). You dream of heaven where "God shall wipe away all tears from their eyes; and there shall be no more death, neither sorrow, nor crying, neither shall there be any more pain" (Rev. 21:4). So, you dream, but you always have; especially since you became a Christian. God still hears you when you pray; he always has. The atom (the very word means indivisible) has been smashed, and the high school physics book you studied has been proved false, but the Bible that you studied in Sunday School has stood the test of science and of time. The basic building blocks of the kingdom of God—faith, hope, and love—the triumvirate of imperishables, are still unbroken. They lift your soul toward God; they always will.

This all being true, then what has changed? You have; I have, and how we fight against the very thought of it!

We have changed physically, though not mentally, certainly not spiritually. We are still young in mind and in spirit, but we are not young in body. This is not to say that many of us are like Stuart Hamblen's old house—"Ain't agonna need this house no longer/Ain't agonna need this house no more," but parts of the house are getting weaker. Incidentally, Hamblen wrote this song made famous by Rosemary Clooney some years ago after discovering the body of an old miner in his tumbledown shack in the High Sierras of California. The song has had special appeal for me because the old miner's shack was located just a few miles from my own mountain cabin. It has even greater appeal for me as I hear Stuart Hamblen sing it. He knew what he wanted to say; Clooney didn't. Hamblen was trying to get across in words and music what Paul said in the most glorious prose ever written: "For we know that if our earthly house of this tabernacle were dissolved, we have a building of God, an house not made with hands, eternal in the heavens" (2 Cor. 5:1).

The sooner we admit that we are getting old, the sooner we shall gain a decisive victory over our own selves; the quicker we shall achieve serenity.

Yes, there are those among us who fight the notion of old age with a reckless intensity. Let me give a case history.

I was writing a series of Sunday School lessons and I introduced one with these three paragraphs.

"Many years ago a young pastor was driving his automobile. His passenger was a little white-haired lady who was known in her church as 'Mother Guinn.' To the young pastor, she represented all that a Christian ought to be. She was completely devoted to Christ. She was calm, serene, bending now and then with the stress of living, but never breaking. And she was wise with a wisdom which came from God. On an impulse the pastor turned to his companion and said, 'I'll be glad when I get to be your age, because then I won't have to fight temptation so hard.'

"Quietly the sixty-year-old woman answered: 'What makes you think that I do not have to fight temptation? In some ways my temptations are greater than ever before.'

"The pastor is no longer young. Now, he is slightly older than was his passenger on that day so long ago. The years have brought to him this truth: There *are* temptations which come to persons of every age. They crash upon the soul with the force of storm-driven waves. Sometimes they come quietly, like termites eating at the floor sills of a house. But they *do* come."

Do you see anything wrong with those paragraphs? I really thought they were somewhat uplifting. I intended them to be. But a women's class in a large Texas church thought otherwise. The members were insulted. They appointed one of them to be a hatchet person to do a job on me. That, she did. She cut off my literary head and threw it in my bloody face. She began her letter: "How ridiculous can you get?" That was the mildest statement in it.

Perhaps at this point I should explain that my assignment included a lesson called *The Sexes in Responsible Relationship*. In this lesson I referred to "human sexuality." The letter writer did not like to see that word used, anywhere. She denied that it had any application to senior adults. She may have lost her own sexuality—I have no way of knowing—but I still have mine. It is worrisome to me sometimes, but I am not ashamed of it. God made me that way.

Lest I be misunderstood, it was perfectly legitimate for the class to take issue with the subject matter or with its treatment, but that was not the main objection in the letter. Can you guess what it was? They did not like it because I had said that the little woman in the young preacher's car was *white-haired* when she was just sixty years old! It so happened, though it was not stated, that I was the young pastor involved, and Mother Guinn was my beloved and her hair *was* white, just as I said. Furthermore, God made her that way. The letter writer informed me that all the women in their class dyed their hair, and she implied that every woman who was sixty should do so, otherwise she was a fool.

My own wife is just one year younger than I. I can count the gray hairs in her brown hair, but if she should want to have those twenty-five gray hairs colored, it is her own business. I guarantee that I would love her just the same!

Yes, Stuart Hamblen, this old house is agrowin' old, but putting a little paint on the roof will not stay the process. How we do try to kid ourselves!

You know what a placebo is—that medicineless pill that the physician prescribes for the hypochrondrical patient who has to be deluded or he will be truly ill. The pill may be of powdered sugar. It can do no good at all. Of course, ordinarily, it can do no harm. I am going to invent a term now that I have never heard used. I shall call what I have in mind, a "psychological placebo." I have a whole mental medicine cabinet full of such sometimes dangerous pills—taken without prescription. Here is placebo number one: "I am just as young as ever." I took one of those pills three years ago and wound up in the intensive care cardiac unit of our hospital. I tried to prove to myself that I was just as strong physically as I was at forty. My doctor of a quarter of a century charged me a hundred and forty dollars for his hospital services at that time. Then, when I had somewhat recovered after a week or so, he gave me strong medicine for which he did not charge me one cent. "You are on that bed today," he said, "because you are stupid. You played the fool. Try admitting to yourself that you are an old man." He put his stethoscope into his little black box and left me to stew in the juice of my own misery. I was then sixty-nine.

## We Must Accept Our Age

Paul Tournier, the great Swiss doctor and psychologist, who stimulates my own thinking on the subject more than does any other writer, objects to this statement as being too "vague." I am sure that to a learned practicing psychologist the term is too simplistic and lacking in precision. For my purpose, however, the terminology is what I want. I am simply zeroing in on one thought: We must accept the *fact* of our age. I am persuaded that once that is done further implications will take care of themselves.

All of us have seen men and women who thought that they could thwart old age by denying that it was happening to them, by trying to by-pass it, by running from it, by attempting to camouflage it, and hiding it from themselves and others. They have tried to hold on to youth by imitating it. They have caricatured themselves and have become the laughing stock for others of whatever age. Instead of by-passing their hated time in life, they have wound up by being by-passed themselves, not by time, which is inexorable, but by all others whom they chance to meet. They were rejected by the young as being dishonest; they were ignored by the old as being silly. In trying to fit themselves where they did not belong, they became misfits everywhere.

Most of us remember a dance called the jitterbug. It was a wild and wacky sort of thing, a series of progressive explosions of syncopated gymnastics. Only the young could manage such physical dexterity. I never tried it. In fact, the only time I ever danced in my whole life was when I stepped barefooted on a coal by a Boy Scout campfire. The jitterbug was a sedate waltz compared to some of the frenzied contortions and unrhythmic acrobatics of what modern youth call dancing. The other night I happened to turn on my television set just as a jostling crowd of young people was committing musical mayhem and terpsichorean sacrilege in the name of "dancing." Before I could switch channels, the young people cleared off a place on the floor and an old woman put on a "demonstration." She tried to imitate their sacroiliac gyrations and they applauded, not her performance, but her obscenity. She reminded me of a molting, fat, old goose waddling around a flock of cackling bantam chickens. I prefer the goose.

Of course that example is extreme and no reader of this book—or would the writer—ever engage in an act like that. It hurt my arthritis just to write about it. But I also know that we can try to reject our age in other, more insidious, and sometimes unconscious ways. To accept one's age means more than just admitting it. It means something more than the resigned fatalism of "I will because I have to." It means saying yes to this blessed time of life when each of us comes nearer than ever before to being the "master of our fate" as the poet Henley said. Accepting one's age means being in harmony with one's self. In keeping with the purpose of this book, it means keeping one's place in the ongoing stream of life. Instead of withdrawal, it means integration. It means, for most of us, just going on unruffled and unafraid, pursuing the constructive purposes of the soul.

To catalog the ways that we can try to contravene the erosions, abrasions, and corrosions of our later years is as futile as is the legalistic approach to Christianity. Christianity is not the matter of keeping laws but is the commitment of the heart to Christ. It is saying yes to him in love and in faith. That done, all else falls into line without the conscious practice of a set of rules, regulations, or rituals.

We say yes to age, not by a refusal to dye our

hair, but by using God's gracious gift of extended years for the betterment of mankind. This is positive acceptance, not negative denial.

### We Must Share Our Age

"Our society is sick." I have put that statement in quotation marks simply because they are the opening words of Paul Tournier's thesis, *An Impersonal Society*. He goes on to say, "The symptoms are localized, but they disclose a disease of the whole organism. Such grave symptoms ought to impel us towards a radical rethinking of the bases of society."

The reason I mentally questioned the quote marks bracketing the first four words is that every theologian, every psychologist, every sociologist, every economist, in short, just about everybody within the framework of that sick society, whether learned or uneducated, who has any regard whatsoever for the welfare of mankind, says the same thing.

Tournier concludes his thesis with these words: "In our society the old have no longer any part to play. It is terrible for them to feel themselves discarded. But it is also bad for the younger members of society, who are thus deprived of an influence which is indispensable to their own development. It is unfortunate for the whole body of society to have as it were one of its members amputated. Left without the counter-balance provided by the old, society is impelled into the frenzied whirl of youth. Everyone is in a rush, everything is urgent, and no one has time to think about the overall problems. Until the day comes when suddenly these feverish toilers stumble into the void. The old must be given a valid place once again in our world" (*Learn to*

*Grow Old,* Harper and Row, p. 77).

When I read these words, my mind immediately leaped to a tragic Old Testament story.

King Solomon was dead. He had built the kingdom of Israel to the greatest glory it had ever achieved. The country was rich beyond compare. It had successfully withstood its enemies without, but there were rumblings within its own government.

Solomon was followed by his weakling son, Rehoboam. Almost immediately a delegation of disgruntled citizens led by Jeroboam who had come from his enforced exile in Egypt, called upon the new king to protest their high taxes. Does that sound familiar in these tax-oppressive days of ours?

Rehoboam "consulted with the old men" and they told him to ease up on his attitudes, to become more the servant of the people rather than their master, then they, in turn, would gladly be his servants forever. Could anyone have improved on this sage advice offered by the men seasoned by the wisdom of experience and much thought? Then the Bible adds:

"But he forsook the counsel of the old men, which they had given him, and consulted with the young men that were grown up with him" (2 Kings 12:8). What was the half-baked advice of these worldly-wise young men? They told the king to swing his tax club a little harder, to let the people know in no uncertain terms who was the boss. They even advised him to throw a little political mud on the memory of his father. Does that sound like modern politics?

Rehoboam listened to the young advisers. They were telling him what he wanted them to say. He levied even higher taxes and when he sent his favorite tax collector, Adoram, to make the collections, that unfortunate man was stoned to death.

In this biblical chapter and the four which follow it there is the record of the breakup of the nation and the degradation of its people.

Government needs the advice of its older citizens. They, more than any other group, understand what Tournier calls "the bases of society." By illustration, an equitable society must be based upon the moral and spiritual precepts of God. These principles may not be recognized as biblical, but they must be present in the conception and administration of a government of the *people*—the emphasis Lincoln is said to have given vocally in his famous Gettysburg Address. A government to endure must be based on the solidarity of its homes. Perhaps nothing so disturbs older people today than does the dreadful knowledge that our homes are breaking up, that countless young lovers are discarding marriage in favor of cohabitation without benefit either of church or state. Hear an old man (by his own confession) again. In another place Tournier says:

"Psychology has become a technique, and the same has happened to medicine, so sociology, to politics, to art and to economics. We think every problem can be solved if only we acquire a sufficiently high technical qualification. Young people read learned tomes about the technique of sex, without realizing that they are being taught everything except how to love; for loving is not a technical skill, it is a personal commitment" (*Learn to Grow Old*, p. 40).

Thus the man of experience in life, thought, and

love gives the foundation of the home, the bedrock of society, *Love*.

We have the technology to put a man on the moon and count his heartbeats a quarter of a million miles away. Through our medical know-how we have seen the last case of smallpox—the bane of our youth—banished from the earth. By our better understanding of the laws of physics we have been able to put together enough atomic, hydrogen, and cobalt bombs to destroy the earth and all that lives thereon. When can we learn to love? When can we tune our hearts to each other? When can we hear the heartbeats of the man next door?

Whatever else my own years have finally taught me, I have learned to love not only myself, my family, and my devoted friends but also the passing stranger who looks at me with eyes that are dead because he sees no hope.

Because of this I want to share my age which, I believe, has given me more understanding, more charity, more forbearance, more patience, and even more faith in the God who rules in the lives of men.

How about you, who may have learned ever so much more?

# 10
## Koinonia

May I invite you to join me in an imaginary trip back through time?

Jesus and his disciples are climbing the rocky trail up the mountain toward the arrogantly pagan city of Caesarea Philippi. Now and then they pause to wipe the blinding sweat from their sunburned, bearded faces. It has been a long journey by foot from Bethsaida, and they are all bone-tired.

Where the trail breaks around the shoulder of a high volcanic cone, the men stop and look backward down the trail up which they have come. All about the little plateau on which they stand are the rocks, heaved upward in some tremendous convulsion when the earth was young. Now and then the bases of the rocks are touched with color. Clumps of anemones—the "Roses of Sharon"—hide their tiny red faces bashfully and the white "lilies of the field"—narcissus—softly brush the sides of the rocks, but the rocks are always there.

Far below, in the buff-colored valley, the Sea of Galilee glistens like a huge silver heart. Little cities are strung along the Jordan River like beads on a shining thread. Jesus looks at them sadly, remembering the people who are deaf to spiritual things and who clamor only after wonders, miracles, and signs. These are his own, but they have received him not. They have rejected his ministry of love.

Finally he turns his back on the distant lake. As he turns around, the slopes of Mount Hermon with its highest ledges dusted with snow rise before him. His eyes travel upward for a moment and then turn back to his followers. Others have failed to understand his mission. How about these that he has chosen so carefully?

With the suddenness of a clap of thunder echoing from the distant peak he hurls a question at them. Upon their answer hangs the spiritual destiny of the world.

*"Who do men say that the Son of man is?"* (author's italics throughout).

There is a moment of silence. Then the voices break in on him. They tell him that some, like bloody Herod Antipas, believe that he is John the Baptist come back to life, that others believe that he is Elijah, or Jeremiah, or one of the other prophets revisiting the earth.

Now, like a second clap of thunder, the question is no longer general but personal. It is sharply directed to their own hearts and minds.

*"But who do you say that I am?"*

Peter is the first to answer. He almost always is. His voice trembles with emotion as he cries: *"Thou art the Christ, the Son of the living God."*

What a mighty declaration! What a glorious truth! What a confession of faith!

A quick smile comes to the face of Jesus and his eyes are tender with love and satisfaction. He speaks, almost in a whisper. *"Blessed art thou, Si-*

*mon Barjona* [Son of Jona] *for flesh and blood hath not revealed it unto thee, but my Father which is in heaven.*" Then, looking at the rocks near them, most of which are movable by a man, his eyes fix upon Peter for a long moment. He turns back and gazes toward the rugged granite cliffs of Hermon, more than nine thousand feet above them, visible through the whole of Palestine. Finally, he says to Peter: *"And I say also unto thee, That thou art Peter, and upon this rock I will build my church: and the gates of hell shall not prevail against it"* (Matt. 16:13-18, RSV and KJV).

"Thou art Peter, [Greek, masculine, *Petros,* a stone] and upon this rock [Greek, feminine, *Petra* a mighty rock] I will build my church."

Peter—a movable stone; Christ—more immovable than were the white cliffs on the eastern crown of Hermon. As a Westerner, I would liken *petra* to the mother lode, where the body of gold is buried and from which the tiny nuggets find their way into the mountain stream.

Once a seminary professor and I backpacked to a small body of water tucked in a granite pocket in the High Sierras, some thirteen thousand feet above sea level. It was called, with some reason, "Lost Lake." As we sat near the broken shoreline, we were in a jumble of smooth, mammoth boulders. Across the lake the waters washed the foot of a cliff that towered into the sky. My thought stirred. I recounted the preceding thought to my theologue friend. He was unimpressed. "Jesus and his disciples spoke Aramaic. Does that distinction hold true there?" he asked.

I said, "Jim, I only know about a dozen words in Aramaic. I cannot read it. I had only two years of Greek in college, plus what I have studied on my own. Peter believed that the church was built on Christ. If he does not say this in 1 Peter 2:4-6, what does he say? I believe that, too, and that is what is important. That is all that matters about the foundation of the church."

My friend's hearty "Amen!" echoed back from the hillside.

Since this is not a "preaching" book or an exercise in apologetics, I shall leave the matter here except to reaffirm what I believe the Bible teaches: The church rests upon Christ, its unshakable foundation. He built his church during his lifetime on the earth. It exists today, two thousand years later, as his spiritual body in the world. The Bible says that he loved the church and gave himself for it. This poses the question: Can one love him without loving his church—his body? Can we serve him in love without serving his church? Should we forsake the assembling of ourselves together in his name when we are cautioned in his Word not to do so? No Bible believer would answer in the affirmative.

We know that Jesus established his church and to that body of baptized believers, he gave the Commission to go "into all the world, and preach the gospel to every creature," as Mark 16:15 puts it. We know that, according to Matthew, he met again with the disciples on an unnamed mountain in Galilee, keeping a rendezvous that he had made with them before he died upon the cross. He assured them that all power in heaven and earth is his and that he would be with them always as they carried out his orders. Those orders were to teach all nations, to baptize them in his name, and to keep on teaching those baptized all that he had commanded.

This means that Jesus had only one hope that his work would be carried on, and that hope rested in the church. His church cannot possibly carry out such a tremendous commission without organization. It cannot implement such organization without regular and frequent meetings where strength can be gained from God in worship, preaching, baptizing, and teaching. It cannot reach the world unless it mounts a missionary offensive in the name of Christ. It cannot do this without supportive meetings. We know all of this. To be a part of it all gives the greatest meaning to our lives. In such a partnership with God and with each other we find our true direction—our ultimate purpose.

While affirming all this, it is a fact that many senior adults quit attending Sunday School and worship services of the church. There are sometimes painful reasons.

These seniors are not as mobile as they have been in the past. Most of them give up driving by the age of seventy or soon thereafter. They are thus dependent upon others for transportation. City bus services are at their lowest ebb on Sundays. Schedules and routes do not serve the church-goers to advantage. There are long periods of waiting, long blocks of walking. The aging church members may find it impossible to enter and leave the buses because of their high steps. They find it emotionally stressful to keep the impatient bus driver and his more impatient passengers waiting while they slowly and sometimes painfully try to climb inside.

They may not even have the money for bus fare to and from the church building.

Any church is obligated to its senior members to provide transportation for them at least for primary worship services. The older member has the right to insist, if necessary, upon this assistance.

If you are such a disenfranchised church member, I offer this suggestion: Tell your pastor about it. After all, his desk, like Harry Truman's, is where the buck stops. You need not be timid about it. You have borne your load of spiritual work cheerfully through the years. You have supported the program of the church financially as best you could. Speak up. Your pastor loves you sincerely. He will help you. I never knew one who wouldn't; nor would I ever want to know one. You may say, "But he ought to know that already!" Indeed, he should, but sometimes he doesn't. You will find your pastor grateful that you have reminded him of your need and the need of others in your age group. Try it and see if this is not true.

You need not be apologetic. The church needs you as never before. You have probably walked with Christ for many decades. Out of that walk with him has come a deepened experience of grace. That can be your testimony. You have learned to combat sorrow, disappointment, frustration, failure, bodily and mental suffering, and the greatest foe of all—sin and its master, Satan. Every other member of the church faces all these battles of the soul. It is true that the Holy Spirit is the ultimate Comforter, Counselor, and Guide, but it is no less true that he has a way of using those who are touched by him. You say, "But I can do nothing." Is that so?

Let me bring your own pastor front and center again. I have a pastor's heart. I served Baptist churches forty-six years. It seems like only yesterday when they were saying, "He's too young to be a pastor; he is not even old enough to vote," and now, I am too old to be one. Between those two extremities time, for me, passed like the puff of vapor described by James, the pastor at Jerusalem. I failed in many ways, but one thing I can say: When I stepped into the pulpit I did my very best at the time. I tried not to please the congregation but my Lord. It is a solemn, demanding task. I needed all the help I could get in my first sermon and in my last.

Consider this. It is the eleven o'clock hour on Sunday morning. The organ plays a soft prelude, or perhaps the notes of a piano set the mood for worship. The choir, led by the director, files into the loft and remains standing. The pastor, perhaps with an assistant, enters and takes his place on the platform in the place assigned to him. The service begins. Watch your pastor while it proceeds. Before long you will see him looking around at the congregation. You can almost feel his eyes upon you. You can feel it, too, while he preaches. If his sermon has power at all, it will be in part because you helped him. You prayed for him. You listened to him attentively, and he could see it. Your spirit joined his. Strength and support flowed from your heart to his own. Who preached? You did, through him.

Something else. If you think that your pastor is always on a spiritual mountaintop in his own life, you are wrong. He is just a man. Sometimes he is strong; many times he is weak. That mountaintop can turn quickly into a valley of spiritual depression—almost of despair. You see, the pastor and his family are not supposed to have any kind of problems. He visits you when you are sick, but his is not supposed to get sick. He comforts you when you are in sorrow, but he is expected to dismiss his own with a smile. If he ever breaks under the pressure, who helps, through love and understanding, to put him together again? I am not trying in any way to exalt your pastor or to make a hero out of him. Only God can make a hero and only God can recognize one. Remember, I have walked in his moccasins—as the Indians would say. Since I am retired, I cannot be accused of self-serving. I want you to know and to feel that your pastor needs *you*. Since he needs you so much; since he is the shepherd of the flock under Christ, you help your church and the Shepherd when you help your pastor to be, and do, his best.

Now, all other considerations aside, *you* need the fellowship of others who believe in Christ as you do and who are serving him as you are. You will benefit the most even when you give yourself to others. It is a paradox of life that in extending your help to others, you gain far more than you give. Once more, in your later years, you find meaning in your existence. You find renewed purpose. The sweet harmony of faith again sings in your heart. Such notes are always muted by isolation.

There remains this objection which I heard from an elderly friend the other day, and it may be yours as well: "Those church members remember me when I was active, was full of vitality 'til it stuck out of my ears, and was completely sure of myself. Now I can see signs in myself that I am growing senile.

I don't want any of them to see me that way. I want to be remembered as I was, not as I am."

I had thought that in my long tenure as a pastor I had heard every excuse that could be devised about nonchurch attendance, and I started to laugh at him, but his dead seriousness stopped me short. It really was not funny. I suppose that all of us, as seniors, have the fear of senility. In my limited observation, this may be our second greatest fear. We, as Christians, are not afraid of death itself. We may be afraid of the *process* of dying, with what could be pain and invalidism, though not necessarily so. The Bible equates death with sleep. Some of us have lain down 25,000 times, carelessly closing our eyes without the fear that we would not open them in the morning. There is a vital difference, I do recognize. One day or one night we shall lay these tired, worn-out, old bodies down for the last time. Then we shall sleep to open our eyes in the land of endless day, where the sleep called death will be no more.

No, we do not dread that. We do fear, though, a kind of living death, which we call senility. That fear is unreasonable, as most of our fears through life have proved to be. Whether this fear troubles you, I cannot know. I do know, because he told me so, it troubles my friend who quit going to church. I worried some about such a fate overtaking me. In fact my fears surfaced just two days ago, while I was engaged in writing this very chapter.

I wrecked our automobile. In fifty-five years of driving, I had never been in a collision. As a pastor, I drove about 2,000 miles a month on the streets and the freeways of California, where the largest concentration of cars and trucks in the world exists.

Then, with my wife in the car, I had an unavoidable crash which totaled out our good old car. We were not injured and neither was any occupant in the car that I had struck. The automobile responsible for the accident never stopped. I was not cited by the highway patrol officer who investigated.

In presenting my claim to my insurance agent, who has handled my insurance needs, both home and cars, this quarter of a century, I said, "Well, Tony, I guess I am growing senile." I was not more than half-joking. Tony laughed. "Is that what it is? I was wondering why we were paying so many claims against teenage drivers. They are all senile."

Then I remembered an interesting item that I had read in my research for this book. Psychologist Frances M. Carp took the "Senility Index," a compendium of commonly accepted "senile signs" developed by a group of scientists some thirty years ago, and applied it to two groups, one with an average age of seventy-two and the other college students. The result was that the college students actually showed more "senile signs" than did the older group.

Then, let us quit the counterproductive self-diagnosis of our own imagined "senile signs" and not prognosticate that because we hunted half an hour for our eyeglasses, which were perched on our noses, that we have become senile. That college kid probably could not spell his proboscis, even if he found it.

Without exception all students of the aging process say that senility is not inevitable. It is highly improbable that anyone reading these lines will ever reach that medical stage. Unless we suffer brain damage—and that can be treated by effective new drugs—we can defeat senility if we do just two things: if we keep our minds active and centered upon something outside ourselves and if we keep social contact and fellowship with others.

Now, back to the objection that we will be looked upon with disfavor simply because we cannot be as active in church as we once were. That is not true either. Why? Because in the church we are in a fellowship of love. Why? Because we will be walking, as in the past, with those who believe and practice the Word of God. The Bible says (and this was directed from the older man, Paul, to the younger man, Timothy): "Rebuke not an elder, but entreat him as a father; and the young as brethren; The elder women as mothers; the younger as sisters, with all purity. Honour widows that are widows indeed" (2 Tim. 5:1-3). Where better than in the church can one find these attitudes?

I would be thoughtless, even heartless, if I did not mention those who simply cannot get to church at all. They are confined to bed, perhaps to wheelchairs. The only contact that they can have with the members of their church is for those members to show enough concern and love to regularly visit them. Thousands upon thousands of retired persons who are committed to Christ find this to be their most rewarding avenue of service. I know. Have you found this out as I have?

Back to the premise of this chapter. The church rests eternally upon Christ. The majestic old song that we have sung all our lives is true: "The Church's one foundation is Jesus Christ her Lord." It is also true that the spiritual house called the church is built up out of living stones, ourselves, the members of it (1 Pet. 2:5).

What a glorious partnership!

As stated in the preface, this has been, intentionally, a very personal book. It has not been written authoritatively, but lovingly, in friendship. It has been written by one who readily admits his own deficiencies, fears, as well as his bright hopes. Much of it, perhaps too much, has been written lightly, that we might laugh together, as friends should. Some is deadly serious, as life itself is serious. I may have written poorly, but I have been honest with myself and with you.

Will you allow me one last testimony before I close this final chapter? The words reveal only a small part of what the church means to me.

February 1, 1974, I retired as pastor of Baptist Temple, San Jose, California, a post that I had held for twenty-two years. To add to my trauma, I was giving up the pastorate itself after nearly a half century. I was sixty-seven, had tried three times to retire, but remained at the insistence of my beloved church, until a new pastor could be called.

That night I almost wore the bedsheets out with my twisting and turning. I wore my patient wife out in the same process. She could not sleep because of my restlessness. Finally, I got up, went into my study, and tried to read. I read one page half a dozen times before giving up. At least, though, Ina was able to get some sleep. At daylight I left a note for her on the breakfast table, got in the car, and drove the six miles to the church building. I let myself into the auditorium. I stood for long moments in the half-light, looking around, the sickness in my stomach gradually infusing my whole body. This was the moment of truth. I was out!

I moved to the rostrum, climbed up the steps, and went behind the pulpit stand. It seemed to be unreal, as though if I but touched the smooth wood of its ledges, the whole thing would fade away. Dimly I remembered that the beautiful piece of church furniture had been built by an expert cabinetmaker in our church, gone now for more than a dozen years, I could almost see his ghostly hands giving the final rubbed finish to the smooth-textured wood until it was like velvet. He seemed to be saying to me, "Go ahead and preach, I'm listening."

A cold shiver touched my back and climbed up to my hair. I sat down weakly on the small padded pew that I had occupied every Sunday. I had to be alone, to pray and to think. A psychologist might say that I was being masochistic—punishing myself for some inverted pleasure that it brought. That would not have worried me much, since I am persuaded that any psychologist who tried to analyze me would wind up jumping off a bridge in his own despair. I was simply filling a deep psychic need, totally unrelated to self-flagellation. I had to pull myself together. I did not need a psychologist or psychoanalyst with his high-flown theories. I needed God. I needed the gift of him who said, "My peace give I unto you." I needed to have my sense of desolation lifted. I needed to have my newfound burden of loneliness alleviated. I needed to find, in a world that was fast receding from me, a stable footing for my faltering feet. I needed to find myself.

My gaze wandered around the room. To the left of the choir loft were two rooms, one above the other. The lower, opening into the auditorium, was used as an office; the upper room, behind the unbroken wall, was once my study. I remembered that day when the building was under construction and I stood on the subfloor of that room, with my own hammer in my hand. As I took a "breather" I watched a deacon carpenter at work. He was carefully sanding the sill of a clerestory window high above the floor of the auditorium, and at my own level. Bill Hightower, as were a score of others that day, was donating his time. I spoke to him. "Bill, you are taking too much trouble with that. Who can see the top of that sill when it is sixteen feet above floor level?" Bill's answer was, "God can see it. This is his house." Not long afterwards Bill was killed in a car wreck. He moved into God's mansion.

In my memory I could see other men and women hard at work for three years of extra time, building the house of worship. Those were the days of pioneer work in California, when Southern Baptists were just getting started, and they could not hire their building built. Many of those my memory brought back were now dead.

I looked out over the empty pews. I could visualize the individuals who sat in their accustomed places every Sunday. The days of family-owned pews has long since vanished, but every pastor who has prayed for the worship hour in his church, has been able to see the members of his congregation as he prayed. They always sat in the same locations. It was as though they obeyed some unwritten law of the Medes and Persians that could never be changed. As I thought of these people, and there had been thousands of them through the years, I remembered their warmth, their love for each other, and I was thankful that their love included me. No matter where I might ever be, I would never be isolated from their love.

I thought of Paul, writing to the beloved church in Philippi, and his remarkable words: "I have you in my heart" (Phil. 1:7). No one knows what Paul really said. He wrote in Greek and the sentence can be translated two ways: either, "I have you in my heart," or, "You have me in your heart." That is the way it should be. The members carry their pastor in their hearts, and he carries them in his own. God intended the love to work both ways.

Then another truth broke through to my mind. No matter where I might find myself, in whatever town, in whatever city, in whatever land, I could find spiritual communities where strangers would instantly become my friends. They would love me not for what I am, but in spite of my flaws and shortcomings; in spite of the way I happened to be dressed; whether or not I had to walk to church services or drove up in a Cadillac. They would love me because of the *koinonia,* a Greek word meaning fellowship, or, as spiritualized and commonly used, "fellowship of believers."

I had found my peace.